sentence combining

English Department

Consulting Editors:
Gregory Cowan and Elisabeth McPherson,
Forest Park Community College

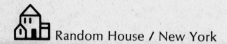 Random House / New York

WILLIAM STRONG
UNIVERSITY OF ILLINOIS

sentence combining

A COMPOSING BOOK

Library of Congress Cataloging in Publication Data

Strong, William, 1940–
    Sentence combining.
        1.   English language—Rhetoric.   I.   Title.
PE1408.S7713   808'.042   72-12864
ISBN 0-394-31703-3

Manufactured in the United States of America. Composed by Cherry Hill Composition, Pennsauken, N.J.

Designed by James M. Wall

First Edition

8B97

for
my folks
whose words still whisper
in my inner ear
and here

acknowledgments

Giving birth to a book is a labor of love and pain. It is conceived in the dark midnight hours when most sensible people are asleep, and it develops for months, even years, before it reaches the black-and-white of printed reality.

With *Sentence Combining: A Composing Book*, the midwives have been many: lots of students, many student teachers, and several instructors experienced in the arts of written discourse, the late Francis Christensen among them. These friends have grunted and giggled over the materials and offered both constructive criticism and encouragement. Because I can't thank them all individually, I would simply like to thank them collectively for their help. They know who they are, and I do too.

Three midwives, however, deserve special acknowledgment. The first is Dr. Richard L. Larson, who gave the manuscript a close, thoughtful reading and provided a number of useful suggestions. The other two are Elisabeth McPherson and Greg Cowan, the Editorial Consultants for Random House who were in on the initial talk about a project for sentence-combining explorations—this deep in the dark of 1968. Since then, Liz and Greg have teased, cajoled, encouraged, harassed, and humored me from the labor of love stage to the completion of the project. They are the kind of midwives who work harder than they should, and if the book has utility it is due largely to their gentleness and friendship.

Kudos, finally, for my wife, Carol, who was patient and insightful, and for Kristin and Eric, who said it was okay to miss a picnic sometimes. *Sentence Combining* is partly theirs.

contents

phase two

Introduction 157

EXPLORATIONS

a note to students

Sentence Combining is a book with a simple aim: to help you strengthen your writing skills and get a feel for some of the stylistic choices available to you in written English. The exploration involves an approach called sentence combining. Simply put, you will investigate the *variety* of ways to say things in English; your search will be for multiple answers (or options) rather than for a single "right" answer.

But this book is *not* a grammar book full of diagrams and terminology. Nor is it a usage book full of prescriptions on "correctness." Nor is it a rhetoric book full of admonitions on organization and such matters. It won't even give you advice on how to write a term paper, fix a fragment, use a comma, undangle a participle, make a footnote, fold an envelope, pass an exam, or get a job. All that is in other books.

How Does It Work?

As the title says, this is a *composing* book. And composing means *doing* writing, not just talking about it. So this is a practical book—a book in which "talk about" writing is not substituted for what you do. No one learns to swim by sitting on the bank, listening to the coach, and playing it safe. The same is true for riding motorcycles, skiing, playing the guitar, talking, making love, building a kite, reading, hanging sheet rock, sewing, or organizing the block for political action. Skills are acquired through experience and practice—through *doing*.

If you've already flipped through the book, you've noticed lists of sentences similar to this one:

MAIN DRAG, SATURDAY NIGHT

1. The cars come cruising up Broadway.
2. The cars are glittering.

3. The paint is harsh.
4. The paint is metallic.
5. The paint is highly waxed.

6. There is a rumble of exhaust.
7. The rumble is great.

8. Lights explode softly off the scene.
9. The lights are for the street.
10. The scene is primitive.

Some of the lists are quite long; others, like this one, are less than twenty sentences. But all the sentences within the lists are short and simple. They are unmodified "basic" sentences—something the new grammarians call *kernel sentences*.[1] Your task (explained in more detail in the Introduction to Phase I) will involve combining the kernel sentences into more readable prose. To do this, you'll use the sentence-combining facility that you *already* possess. In other words, you won't "study" grammar; instead you'll use the resources that were "programmed" into your brain by the time you were six years old. These resources, plus some practice, will enable you to *transform* these kernel sentences into fairly sophisticated sentences and paragraphs.

For the "Main Drag, Saturday Night" paragraph you might come up with some transformations that look something like these:

TRANSFORMATION 1

The glittering cars come cruising up Broadway. Their paint is harsh, metallic, and highly waxed. There is a great rumbling of exhaust. Street lights explode softly off the primitive scene.

TRANSFORMATION 2

The cars that glitter come cruising up Broadway. Their metallic paint is harsh and highly waxed. There is a great rumble of exhaust. Lights on the street explode softly off the scene—which is primitive.

Or you might come up with different variations—other transformations based on what sounds right to your ear.

The point is this: since there are many ways to say things in English, your skill in writing depends on whether you can "see"—and *choose from*—the various possibilities available to you. This process of selection, of "turning phrases," is something that writers have taught themselves to do. It is hoped that this book will teach you the same thing and will make you sensitive to the options.

The explorations are organized to proceed from short lists to longer ones. As the lists become longer, more difficult transformations —those that mark the styles of skilled or professional writers—will be introduced. The steps are gradual, however, so that you'll have little, if any, difficulty. In each exploration, you'll be given the content of what to say; your job is to say it the best way you can, making a longer

[1] Some sentences in the lists aren't kernels, in the strict sense of the word. But because most are, and because we're more interested in combining the sentences than in analyzing them, we'll use the word "kernel" anyhow. It may occasionally be technically inaccurate, but it's handy.

sentence out of several short ones. Since the spelling is there for you to copy, the only technical detail you'll need to figure out for yourself is punctuation.

Often, if you follow the Suggestions, you'll compose on your own. Usually you'll be asked to extend the development of an idea or a description, or to react to it in some way. By doing the Suggestions regularly and saving your papers, you can see how these activities are improving your writing.

After Phase I you'll move into the Phase II explorations. Here you'll extend your sentence-combining facility in a more systematic and disciplined way by imitating the structures that professional writers use. Phase II is designed to help you see the "architecture" of more elaborate sentences, thus adding to the skills you've acquired in Phase I. After Phase II, with your skills at the level of *awareness*, you'll be on your own.

What Good Will It Do?

Sentence Combining has evolved from some important educational research.[2] The research concluded that students who worked with exercises in sentence combining produced an increase of 32 percent in "critical transform types"—the kinds of structures that seem to mark skilled writing. With some deliberate practice, then, you should be able to increase your own transforming skills in a fairly dramatic way.

In addition to better sentences, however, there should be another payoff. You'll notice that your explorations have been designed to result in paragraphs or short papers. The design is intentional. Writing is a matter of putting sentences into "meaning units" called paragraphs. You'll see the patterns of organization in the paragraphs—patterns that you can employ in your independent writing. You'll be "transforming" sentences but you'll also be building paragraphs. The two operations go on simultaneously in the mind of any writer. You'll find that this book will help you develop a feel for both sentence structure and paragraph organization.

[2] John Mellon, *Transformational Sentence-Combining: A Method of Enhancing the Development of Syntactic Fluency in English Composition* (Champaign, Ill.: National Council of Teachers of English, 1969). The significance of this research has recently been confirmed by Dr. Frank O'Hare in his 1971 doctoral dissertation titled *The Effect of Sentence-Combining Not Dependent on Formal Knowledge of a Grammar on Student Writing.*

Sentence Combining is a skill-building text. It won't help you find something to say when you're asked to write a research paper nor will it offer rules about organization, style, usage, diction—the matters that composition books often take up. Its main purpose is to help you "hear" the stylistic options available to you and to help you "see" patterns of development, both in sentences and paragraphs. You'll probably find the skills more useful than any number of "rules."

What Are the Assumptions?

Now that you understand the design of the program, you may be interested to know something about the assumptions on which it is based. You may want to discuss these with your instructor.

The first assumption is that every person who uses a language in his day-to-day life is a language expert. Every language user undergoes an intensive "course" in his native language at a very early age; in a sense, language is his teacher and the environment is his classroom. He acquires his language, of course, without any books, teaching machines, lectures on correctness, drill, or formal study. Learning occurs naturally and painlessly. Simply by being exposed to language and by testing out our responses over a five- or six-year period, we begin to internalize the fantastically complex signaling systems that make up our language. Just *how* this occurs no one knows. About all the linguist can do is make some educated guesses based on his knowledge of language.

The implications of this first assumption are worth noting. To begin with, this book can't *teach* you anything "new" about language. All it can do is make you somewhat more consciously *aware* of what you've already learned through years and years of experience in encoding and decoding language messages. You have a wealth of linguistic power "beneath the surface." The intensive exploration of sentence combining is one way of bringing some of those resources to the level of awareness so that they can be used deliberately and effectively.

A second assumption is that a technical knowledge of grammar will have little or no impact on your ability to use the language with grace and precision, any more than the knowledge of physics will make you a Grand Prix racing champion or a knowledge of chemistry will make you a gourmet chef. Car racing depends on nerve and reflexes; cooking depends on taste and imagination. Writing depends on our ability to use language, not on our ability to describe it. The reason for this is simple: analysis is a process of taking apart; synthesis is a process of putting together: Writing is, of course, a process of putting together and "composing yourself," so to speak.

In *Sentence Combining*, then, almost all your attention will be focused on synthesis—how sentences combine—rather than on analysis. You'll focus on the *operations* of sentence combining, not on the kernel sentences themselves. These operations are beneath the surface and therefore need to be explored. So the aim isn't to diagram individual sentences, to name parts, or to memorize and recite "rules" for sentence combining; it's simply to explore the patterns that make for choices in written English. Such a focus will probably lead you to write longer sentences with increased modification, and that's good, since length and modification are two marks of language growth. But you'll also learn how to tighten your writing, and that's good too.

A third assumption is that speech is the primary, or basic, language system and that writing is a secondary system, based on speech. Linguists have shown that historically, culturally, and physiologically speech always precedes writing. You already know, of course, that compared to talk a piece of writing is limited and inefficient. Alphabet letters don't always match speech sounds; sentence and paragraph punctuation can't fully convey the meanings signaled by loudness, pause, or the lift of an eyebrow; writing has to proceed one thing after another, left to right, and down the page, whereas the organization of speech is much more fluid. Yet skill in the secondary system, writing, is one of the main cultural tattoos that mark "educatedness" in our society. Most of us have to live in a reality in which we are judged "able" or "not able" on the basis of our facility in written English. It's possible to debate whether such judgments are fair or right, but the judgments are still there. Good writers are those who make "connections" between their talk and their writing; your exploration of transforms will help you discover a wide variety of such connections.

You may find the process of transforming (or sentence combining) is a bit more deliberate and difficult in writing than in talking, since in speech the process seems almost automatic. *The point, though, is that the process of transforming is basically an oral process because speech is the primary system.* And since transforming is basically oral, you must do the *Sentence Combining* exercises *aloud*—or at least whispered to yourself. You must *hear* the transformed sentences. From the various possible options, you select the sentence that sounds best to your ear. According to reports, this is what successful writers actually do.

You must also *take your time* with the explorations. Being aware of the mental process that your brain goes through in transforming sentences is one thing; but you've also got to listen for what some people call the "music" of written language—a music with rhythms different from those of speech. This may sound like a strange suggestion, especially when everyone seems to be pressuring you to read faster. And you're probably not used to "slow" transformation, which amounts to exploring different ways of "saying" the same thing in a controlled situation. But almost inevitably this kind of slowdown tends to speed up the process of acquiring "sentence sense," a kind of gut feel for the flow of different kinds of prose.

Re-reading is what really helps in developing this "feel." In addition to playing with transformations and making their choices, professional writers also seem to spend considerable time hearing the way sentences fit together to make up the "melody" of their writing. They listen for the dips and swaying curves of some phrases, the hard, rhythmic, regular punch of others. They sensitize themselves to avoid sentences where meaning is almost obscured within the lengthy confines of the sentence itself; they study those sentences where pause, and momentary reflection, have their impact. So you'll have to take time and listen closely to your explorations.

The point of all this is that everything in the secondary system of writing has its effect, and skill in composing comes from an awareness of these effects (a sense of audience) and a deliberateness in manipulating or choosing the effects (a sense of purpose). Your task is to hear the available transformed sentences, to become aware of the options.

There are really no right or wrong answers, no external rules to follow. The rules for language—for speech—are already built into your brain. Your transformations follow the rules, and as you go through this book you'll make use of them in increasingly systematic, patterned, and sophisticated ways. Some minor conventions of writing, such as where to put commas, will come out in class discussion; you can learn about those things when you need to. After all, you've got the mental resources to transform basic patterns into millions of structures which no human being has ever uttered before but which are intelligible, nevertheless, to other users of the language. And if you're on top of all that, what's a convention or two?

a note to teachers

An *Instructor's Manual* for *Sentence Combining: A Composing Book* is available to you from Random House, free. If you don't have your copy yet, write to the College Department, Random House, Inc., 201 East 50th Street, New York, N.Y. 10022.

The *Manual* explains the research-based rationale for the program, offers teaching suggestions, and provides transparency masters in an 8 x 10 format. From these masters, it's a simple matter to prepare your own acetate transparencies for an overhead projector. The use of these visuals (or ones of your design) is strongly recommended as a basic in-class approach to stimulate exploration of stylistic options—the variety of ways to say things in written English. In writing laboratories, transparencies will provide new material for students to work with.

The *Manual* emphasizes that this program of sentence combining should be viewed as a skill-building *adjunct* to a regular composition program; in no sense, however, is it a grammar book. The focus of this text is on style, the developing of more sophisticated and varied sentence patterns. The exercises provide the content and organization for paragraphs and short papers. The student's job is to transform "kernel sentences" in the best way he can; the teacher's job is to open discussion on why one transform works well, another less well. Some discussion of writing conventions will naturally emerge from work with transforms, but the main emphasis should be on making choices from stylistic options. This means developing "sentence sense" by playing with alternatives, turning phrases, hearing new possibilities. It doesn't mean drill or the naming of sentence parts.

Because the point of the book is to offer students experience and practice in combining sentences that might actually occur, rather than in analyzing the deep structure of English, the basic units are some-times not *kernels* in the strict sense of the word. For example, passives, questions, and some modifying combinations are already transformed, partly to save the student from doing unnecessary work and partly to keep the basic units reasonably close to ordinary constructions. Some "modified" kernels are presented to force attention to large syntactic units such as phrases and clauses. Until large numbers of professional writers publicly assert that technical grammatical terminology is inval-uable to their art, an emphasis on performance and useful exploration should more than compensate for liberties taken with the definition of a linguistic term such as "kernel."

For the same reason, pronouns are variously dealt with. Often, especially early in the text, a group of kernels will repeat the noun headword, thus giving the student the chance to put pronouns where they'll fit best. The smooth and skillful handling of pronouns in long sentences is something many students need to practice. At other times, especially later in the text, the pronoun substitutions have already been made. Coordinators and subordinators also appear occasionally in the kernels, especially in early exercises. As students get more expert at transforming sentences, it will be easier for them to supply their own connectors; at the end of Phase I almost the only ones given are those necessary to avoid completely awkward sentences.

In addition to focusing on sentences, however, the text also presents patterns of paragraph organization that can be discussed in class. It's recommended that these strategies of organization—whether narrative, descriptive, argumentative, or expository—be approached inductively so that students have an opportunity to compare notes and make their own generalizations. Many of the exploration activities in Phase I have suggestions for further writing, and sometimes ways of organizing can be copied or extended. This seems to be a rather painless way for many students to learn a new "voice" or style of writing.

This book, then, is one of synthesis and sentence play. At first a good number of your students will probably produce elaborate and disastrously convoluted sentences. Do not panic. This is a stage of Phase I. The process of elaboration and sentence expansion is, of course, a first step in the generative process; the next step is tightening and compressing, making the prose more lithe and muscled. Students soon discover that not all options are equally satisfactory. "A crisp, tempting salad" is usually better than "A crisp salad which is tempting." In the same way, "The young developing writer works with options" somehow seems better than "Options are worked with by the young writer who is developing."

First the exploration and manipulation, then a sense of style and rhetorical possibilities: this is what *Sentence Combining* is all about.

phase
one

introduction

Phase I of *Sentence Combining* involves lists of basic, unmodified, kernel sentences. By combining these kernels, you'll begin to see just how many choices you, as a writer, actually have. You'll need to understand two terms: *kernel sentences* and *transformations*. When you know the terms, you know what the program is all about.

Kernels, or basic sentence patterns, are structures that many linguists believe are used over and over in language. The kernel is a kind of fixed formula or frame that the brain uses when sending or receiving messages. The *patterns* of kernels are unchanging, but the *messages* expressed by the patterns can differ. For example:

Writers eat fish.
Fish eat writers.

The pattern is the same, and so are the words, but the message is different.

There aren't many of these basic kernel patterns. English has between four and ten, depending on whose book (and whose system for explaining kernels) you are reading. Yet these four, or even ten, basic patterns generate billions of sentences, each unique, understandable, and recognizable as English. How?

This huge variety of sentences comes about through *transforming*. A transformation is a process or operation that combines the basic patterns into longer, more complex structures. Like the number of kernels, the number of these transforming operations is fairly limited; and like kernels, the transformations are systematic. And a good thing, too, for if there were huge numbers of kernels and huge numbers of transforms, learning a language would really be a chore, perhaps even impossible.

We can think of the transforming processes as the rules of language that have been programmed into the computer of the human mind. Some of the rules are relatively simple, such as adding /s/, /z/, and /iz/ sounds to nouns as a way of showing "more than one" (for example, lights, pens, and boxes). Some rules are more complex. You have learned, for example, that a basic kernel sentence such as

1. The writer is young.

can quickly and automatically be transformed into "the young writer."
You have also learned that the basic kernel can undergo further transformations when you add more basic patterns:

1. The writer is young.
2. The writer is developing.
3. The writer works with options.

The new transformations (T) might look like one of these:

T₁. The young, developing writer works with options.
T₂. The young writer who is developing works with options.
T₃. The writer who is young and developing works with options.
T₄. Options are worked with by the young, developing writer.

As you can see, even a short cluster of kernels offers several possibilities; perhaps you can think of others to add to the ones above. The
point is to produce the possibilities, then make choices.
    What happens when we add more kernels to the original cluster?

1. The writer is young.
2. The writer is developing.
3. The writer works with options.
4. The options are stylistic.
5. The options are for insights.
6. The insights are into language.

Suppose we've selected T₁ as the transformation that sounds best. We'll
simply extend it with further transformations:

T₁. The young, developing writer works with options.
T₅. The young, developing writer works with stylistic options for
    insights into language.

There are, of course, several other possibilities. Here are two more;
decide which of the three you prefer.

T₅. The young, developing writer works with stylistic options for
    insights into language.
T₆. The young, developing writer works with options of style for
    language insights.
T₇. The young, developing writer works for language insights through
    stylistic options.

Notice in T₇ that *with* has been changed to *through*; such minor additions or changes are no problem. You're invited, even encouraged, to make such changes—as long as you retain the basic meaning. For example, you might want to change a word like *for* to a phrase like *to gain*:

T₈. The young, developing writer works with stylistic options to gain language insights.

Such choices are up to you. The important thing is to get some sense of the possibilities available as you go through the process of transformation.

To summarize, then: kernels are the basic stuff of sentences; transformations are what we do to put the stuff together. In Phase I you'll be working with transformations, practicing the ways to form more sophisticated and mature sentences.

The Phase I exploration is organized into "strings" of kernel sentences, with each string arranged in "clusters." For instance, "Takeoff" is a string of twelve kernels grouped in four clusters, 1–3, 4–5, 6–8, 9–12. Each cluster of kernel sentences can be transformed into a single sentence.

TAKEOFF

1. A jet rumbles on the runway.
2. The jet is silver-skinned.
3. The jet is sleek.

4. The jet waits for clearance.
5. The clearance is from the tower.

6. The engines begin to wind up.
7. The windup is sudden.
8. The windup is with a roar.

9. The plane powers down the runway.
10. The runway is concrete.
11. The plane lifts against the horizon.
12. The horizon is edged with clouds.

Here are two possible transformations for the first cluster:

T₁. A sleek, silver-skinned jet rumbles on the runway.
T₂. A sleek jet with silver skin rumbles on the runway.

The second cluster can become:

T₁. It waits for the clearance from the tower.
T₂. It is waiting for clearance from the tower.

The next cluster (6–8) can be transformed to read:

T₁. The engines wind up suddenly with a roar.
T₂. The engines begin to wind up with a sudden roar.
T₃. Suddenly the engines wind up with a roar.

The final cluster (9–12) can also be transformed in several ways:

T₁. The plane powers down the concrete runway and lifts against the horizon that is edged with clouds.
T₂. The plane powers down the concrete runway, lifting against the cloud-edged horizon.
T₃. Powering down the concrete runway, the plane lifts against the horizon which is cloud-edged.

Of course, the transforms offered for each cluster are merely samples; there are other possible ways of combining the kernels. As you can see, you can quickly and easily combine the kernels into longer sentences, but if you seriously explore *all* of the possibilities, you must really stretch yourself, calling upon all your linguistic resources.

When you are ready to choose the transforms you like best, it might help you to relax if you remember that there is no single right answer in most linguistic matters. Of course, there is a basic question of whether it makes sense, and perhaps some mechanical matters of spelling and punctuation. But aside from objective meaning, "rightness" in language is almost always related to the situation and the personal preferences of the users.

how to use phase one

1. As you combine sentences, listen to them; say them aloud in several ways; experiment with new structures.
2. In the beginning, at least, write out all the transforms you can think of for each cluster; then choose the one you like best.
3. In a special notebook, write out the final transforms for each string; use the notebook daily.
4. Compare your transforms with those of the other students; discuss which transformations sound best; try to figure out why.
5. Look for the patterns that show up over and over as you make your combinations; you'll also see patterns of spelling and punctuation as you work.
6. Go beyond the lists that are given in the text by following the Suggestions; in other words, *keep writing*.

EXPLORATIONS

FRENCH FRIES

1. French fries are loaded into a basket.
2. The French fries are white.
3. The basket is wire.

4. Then they are lowered.
5. The lowering is slow.
6. The lowering is into oil.

7. Their bath crackles.
8. Their bath foams.
9. The bath is hot.

10. The potatoes release a puff.
11. The potatoes are thinly sliced.
12. The puff is steam.

13. They come out crispy brown.
14. They come out streaked with oil.

☞ NOTE: In "French Fries," sentences 10–12 and 13–14 can be combined into one longer sentence. Some writers consciously try to vary sentence length in their work.

Hamburgers

1. The patties are grayish pink.
2. They are grainy like oatmeal.

3. They have already been laid out.
4. They are on the griddle.
5. The griddle is black.
6. The griddle is old.

7. They begin to sizzle in a puddle.
8. The puddle is greasy.

9. Blood sputters.
10. Blood pops.
11. Blood bubbles away.
12. The bubbling is into oatmeal grease.

13. Their size shrinks.
14. The shrinking is steady.

☞ NOTE: In "Hamburgers," sentences 1–2, 3–6, and 7–8 can be combined into a single sentence. Explore the options to find out whether you like one, two, or three sentences in the 1–8 sequence.

Coffee

1. He sips at his coffee cup.
2. The cup is chipped along the rim.

3. The taste is bitter.
4. The taste is acidic.
5. The taste is faintly soapy.

6. There is a film.
7. The film is brown.
8. The film is on the inside of his cup.

9. He takes extra care.
10. The care is so that he doesn't spill any on his clothes.

11. He is afraid.
12. The fear is that it might eat holes in the material.

Table

1. The table is littered with refuse.
2. The refuse belongs to other people.

3. They have left signatures everywhere.
4. The signatures are stained.
5. The signatures are greasy.

6. He stares at cups.
7. The cups are in a pile.
8. The cups are for coffee.
9. The cups are stained with lipstick.

10. Off to one side is a hamburger.
11. The hamburger is half-eaten.
12. Flies rest there.
13. The flies are nervous.

14. A sign is buried in the garbage.
15. The sign is small.
16. The sign is neatly lettered.

17. He reads the sign.
18. The sign pleads for students to bus their own dishes.

☞ NOTE: In "Table," sentences 14–16 and 17–18 have the same "headword"—the word "sign." This means that you can combine these two groups into one sentence if you wish.

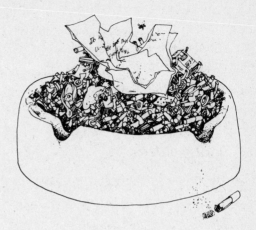

Ashtray

1. The ashtray squats.
2. The ashtray is fat.
3. The ashtray is ugly.
4. The ashtray is in the middle of the table.

5. It is a monstrosity.
6. The monstrosity is porcelain.

7. The insides are blackened.
8. The blackening is with millions of ashes.

9. Into it have been heaped cigarettes.
10. Into it have been heaped crusts of food.
11. Into it have been heaped poems.
12. The poems are written on paper napkins.

13. It accepts all offerings.
14. The acceptance is with indifference.

☞ SUGGESTION: Take a close look at a place where you sometimes eat lunch. Pay special attention to the details of the table, the
food, the silverware—anything that is real and immediate. Write a
description in which you make it real for somebody else.

Matchstick

1. The match is scraped against the box.
2. The scraping is a noise.
3. The noise is raspy.

4. It sputters into flame.
5. The sputtering is uneasy.
6. The flame is yellowish.

7. The flame wavers.
8. The flame trails its way.
9. The way is up the matchstick.

10. Then it dies.
11. Its death is with a sudden puff.

12. A wisp threads upward.
13. The wisp is smoke.
14. The wisp becomes part of the shadows.

Hair

1. Jeff eyed himself in the mirror.
2. He began combing his hair.
3. It was long.
4. It was wavy.
5. It flowed over his ears.

6. He worked the bangs to one side.
7. He stroked them over his eyebrows.

8. Then he pressed his fingertips against his temples.
9. His fingers dug in.
10. They tugged.
11. They straightened the wig.

Street Scene

1. A dude swaggers down the sidewalk.
2. He clicks his fingers to the beat.

3. He is tuned in to music.
4. He is tuned in to verbal hysteria.
5. These come from his radio.

6. The sound jerks ahead of him.
7. It bounces ahead of him.

8. It announces his arrival to the shoppers.
9. It announces his arrival to the storekeepers.
10. It announces his arrival to the girls in the cafe.

11. One girl giggles.
12. She blushes.
13. She tries to look bored.
14. She tries to look very cool.

15. The scene is tense.
16. The scene is clicking.

Patrol

1. Harris checks in at 4:00.
2. Jones checks in at 4:00.

3. They have taken care of the reports by 5:00.
4. They have taken care of the forms by 5:00.

5. Then they hustle downstairs.
6. They hustle through the dispatch office.
7. They hustle into the garage.

8. Their car is gassed up.
9. It is ready for the night's patrol.

10. They wheel out of the station.
11. They wheel into the rush-hour traffic.

12. The radio squawks its coded numbers.
13. It squawks its dispatches.
14. It squawks its orders.

15. They nod to the people they know on the street.
16. They wave to the children.
17. But the evening stretches before them.
18. It stretches uneasily.

☞ SUGGESTION: Consider the last sentences of "Street Scene" and "Patrol." Both paragraphs end on a kind of mysterious edge. See if you can write about what happens next in either scene—or, perhaps, how they may be leading to a third story that combines both scenes.

In Touch

1. Children are remarkable for something.
2. These children are young.
3. The something is an ability.
4. The ability is to remain "in touch."
5. They are in touch with their feelings.

6. They know themselves well.
7. They have not learned to wear masks.
8. Masks cover up feelings.

9. They acknowledge feelings.
10. They show their joy.
11. They show their unhappiness.
12. They show their curiosity.
13. They show their excitement.

14. They do not repress feelings.
15. They have not learned how.

16. They are still in touch.
17. They respond with openness.
18. Their openness is to the world.
19. Their openness is to others.

WAVE

1. Michael is in the crowd.
2. Michael sways from side to side.

3. Michael's voice is the crowd's voice.
4. It is hoarse.
5. It is chanting.
6. It is calling for change.

7. Michael is part of a wave.
8. The wave sweeps past the barricade.
9. The barricade is made of police.
10. The wave flows over the steps.
11. The wave crashes against a door.
12. The wave falls back again.

13. There is another push.
14. The push is harder.
15. The push is from behind.

16. The wave surges forward again.
17. The wave has momentum.
18. The momentum is crushing.

19. There is a scream.
20. The scream shows pain.
21. The scream is anguished.

☞ SUGGESTION: Pick up this story from here and finish it. Try to keep the kind of writing you do as much like these earlier sentences as you can, so it will all fit together.

Main Drag, Saturday Night

1. The cars come cruising up Broadway.
2. The cars are glittering.

3. The paint is harsh.
4. The paint is metallic.
5. The paint is highly waxed.

6. There is a rumble of exhaust.
7. The rumble is great.

8. Lights explode softly off the scene.
9. The lights are for the street.
10. The scene is primitive.

11. The boys are wearing their masks.
12. The masks are sullen.
13. The masks are tough looking.

14. The girls are decked out in hairdos.
15. The hairdos are bizarre.

16. It is like a supercarnival.
17. The supercarnival is spectacular.

18. It is part of our mating rites.
19. The mating rites are weird.
20. The mating rites are national.

Most of Us Remember

1. Most of us remember Groper.
2. We remember from our high school days.

3. He was angular.
4. He was muscled.
5. He had huge hands.

6. The quarterback would send him down.
7. The quarterback would send him out into the flat.

8. And then the football would come.
9. It looped in an arc.
10. The arc spiraled.

11. Groper would go up.
12. He would scramble with the defense.
13. The defense clawed at his jersey.

14. He was always in the right place.
15. He was always there at the right time.

16. Now we all wonder.
17. We wonder about Groper.

18. He just hangs around town.
19. He does odd jobs.

20. You can see him in the evenings.
21. He watches the team.
22. The team practices.

☞ NOTE: In "Most of Us Remember," sentences 16–17 and 18–19 can be combined with a connector like "because."

Just Before the Rain Falls

1. The wind comes up.
2. It bends the trees.
3. The bending is in a rhythm.
4. The rhythm is against the sky.

5. There is a darkening.
6. It is as if the sky were poising itself.

7. Clouds scud across the horizon.
8. The clouds are fat.
9. The clouds are grayish.
10. The scudding is low.

11. A hush gentles the wind.
12. The trees suddenly go still.

13. A boy looks up from his play.
14. The boy is little.
15. He looks at the trees.
16. The trees are no longer making a noise.

17. He feels something on his arm.
18. The something is light.
19. The something is wet.

20. And then it begins to rain.
21. It rains like hell.

Making a Stew

1. George opened a drawer.
2. The drawer was in the kitchen.
3. He took out a book.
4. The book was for recipes.
5. He opened the book.
6. He looked at a recipe.
7. The recipe was for stew.

8. Then he opened a door.
9. The door was to the refrigerator.
10. He took out carrots.
11. He took out potatoes.
12. He took out onions.
13. He took out meat.

14. He picked up a knife.
15. The knife was for butchering.
16. He cut the meat.
17. The meat was red.
18. He cut it into cubes.
19. The cubes were thick.

20. Then he cut the carrots.
21. The carrots were fresh.
22. They cracked under his knife.
23. The crack was sharp.

☞ SUGGESTION: How about helping George with the stew? Watch out when cutting up the onions because they're the strong yellow ones. Work with the feel and smell and color of things.

The Potter

1. The potter works with clay.
2. He is skilled.
3. He sits at his wheel.
4. His brow is wrinkled.
5. The wrinkles show concentration.

6. His hands are slender.
7. His hands are aged.

8. The clay is damp.
9. The clay is earthen.
10. The clay is a mass.
11. The mass is sodden.
12. It resists form.

13. He centers the clay.
14. The clay revolves on the wheel.
15. It is writhing against his hands.

16. He makes an opening.
17. He pierces the mass.
18. The mass is clay.
19. He uses his fingers.
20. He uses his thumbs.

21. His hands lift the clay.
22. The clay becomes a shape.
23. The shape is cylindrical.

24. One hand enters the cylinder.
25. The cylinder is revolving.
26. The other hand pushes against the sides.
27. It works the shape.

28. The sides begin to expand.
29. The expansion creates a bowl.
30. It is ringed with lines.

31. The potter's face is contented.
32. The face is smiling.
33. The smile is tranquil.

34. He has conquered the clay.
35. The wrinkles have vanished.
36. The wrinkles were on his forehead.
37. The vanishing is for the time being.

Working Girl

1. Jan is a working girl.
2. She bounces through a routine.
3. The routine is from 8 to 5.

4. Then she waits for the bus.
5. The bus takes her back.
6. The bus takes her to her apartment.
7. The apartment is uptown.

8. She is now on her own.
9. She is having a great time.

10. Her senses are alive to something.
11. The something is new.
12. The something is delicious.
13. The something is called "freedom."

14. Each day is electric.
15. Each day is exciting.

16. Her face is poised.
17. Her face is proud.
18. Her face smiles with confidence.
19. The confidence is quiet.

20. She has legs.
21. Her legs are long.
22. Her legs are waxy.

23. She has dates.
24. The dates are many.
25. But she is in no hurry.
26. The hurry would be to settle down.

Pawnbroker

1. The pawnbroker moves behind his counter.
2. He surveys his estate.
3. His survey is with cunning.
4. The cunning is like that of a cat.

5. He keeps his eyes glazed.
6. He keeps his eyes bored.
7. This is when he talks.

8. The voice is a whine.
9. The whine is nasal.
10. The whine is reedy.
11. It echoes back to his upbringing.
12. His upbringing was in the Bronx.

13. His face is olive.
14. His face is puffy.
15. It is like a loose rubber mask.

16. But his mind is razor quick.
17. This is as he sizes up customers.
18. The customers wander in from the street.
19. They wander in to bargain.
20. The bargaining is on unclaimed items.
21. The items are in the window.

22. He acts as if he is wounded by each sale.
23. But he makes a profit.
24. The profit is on every transaction.

☞ SUGGESTION: Try to sketch "the essence" of somebody you like or dislike. Notice that the sketch of the pawnbroker has both description and some talk about his background and way of working.

American Unfreeway

1. The cars creep onto the freeway.
2. The cars crawl their way west.

3. Honks anounce the Great Parade.
4. Bleats announce the Great Parade.
5. The Great Parade is to the suburbs.

6. The drivers are hot.
7. The drivers are tired.
8. The drivers are anxious to get home.

9. There is a sign.
10. The sign is on the highway.
11. "Speed 70."
12. Cars move at 5 miles an hour.
13. Then cars move at 15 miles an hour.
14. But no cars go 70.
15. No cars even go 50.

16. Cars stop.
17. Cars start.
18. Cars change lanes.
19. Cars stop again.

20. An announcer croons excitement.
21. The announcer is on the radio.
22. The radio is in the car.
23. The excitement is for a race.
24. The race is the Indianapolis 500.
25. The race will be held this weekend.

26. A thousand spits begin to turn.
27. The spits are in the suburbs.
28. The spits are for barbecues.
29. The spits are electric.

30. Clock-watching wives await.
31. Restless children await.
32. The waiting is for the return.
33. The return is for the Great Provider.
34. The Great Provider is part of the Great Parade.

☞ SUGGESTION: This essay suggests that so-called freeways are not very free. Is the writer talking about other kinds of freedom too? Write an essay showing other ways in which the people using the "freeway" are not "free."

Consumption

1. Statistics can be used.
2. One use is to compute averages.
3. The averages are about Americans.

4. An American is born.
5. A birth occurs every four seconds.
6. This rate of occurrence is an average.

7. This American lives seventy years.
8. Seventy years is an average.

9. And what does one "average American" consume?

10. He consumes food.
11. The food is of all kinds.
12. Some food is packaged.
13. Some food is unpackaged.
14. The amount is 50 tons.

15. He consumes iron.
16. He consumes steel.
17. This consumption is in a form.
18. The form is products.
19. The products include cars.
20. The products include appliances.
21. The products include clips.
22. The clips are for paper.
23. The amount is 28 tons.

24. He consumes 1,200 barrels.
25. The barrels are products.
26. The products are made from petroleum.

27. He consumes fibers.
28. The fibers are for clothing.
29. The amount is 1½ tons.

30. He consumes wood.
31. The wood is used for construction.
32. The wood is used for paper.
33. The amount is about 4,500 cubic feet.

34. The result of this consumption is waste.
35. The waste comes in all forms.
36. Some pollutes the air.
37. Some pollutes the water.
38. Some litters the environment.
39. The waste amounts to about 100 tons.

40. Anyone for population stability?
41. Anyone for population reduction?

☞ NOTE: Do you prefer sentences 40 and 41 combined or stated separately? Why? As a reader, how do you respond to a conclusion that asks a question? How does the effect of a question ending differ from the effect of a summary ending?

THINGS

1. Our culture pushes us to acquire.
2. The acquisition is of things.

3. Things are evidence.
4. The evidence is tangible.
5. The evidence is of our "success."
6. Success is financial.
7. Success is social.

8. We are taught to consume.
9. The consumption is of quantities of things.
10. The teaching is at an early age.

11. This teaching occurs through advertising.
12. Advertising shows "the good life."
13. "The good life" is tied to things.
14. The things are material.

15. Advertising also creates responses.
16. The responses are automatic.
17. The responses are unthinking.
18. The responses are to brand names.

19. Our "need" is therefore shaped.
20. Our "need" is for things.
21. The shaping is done by advertisers.
22. Advertisers manipulate our perceptions.
23. The perceptions are of "success."

24. Advertising thus helps determine the quality.
25. The quality is of culture.
26. The culture is American.

☞ SUGGESTION: Develop either sentences 11–14 or 15–18 in greater detail—that is, with a specific example or two. To do this, thumb through a popular magazine, paying attention to the "messages" that are taught through pictures and text. Relate these specific messages to your writing.

Parable 1

1. A Fox saw a Crow.
2. The Crow was flying.
3. The Crow had some cheese.
4. Her beak held the cheese.

5. The Crow settled on a branch.
6. The branch was on a tree.

7. Fox wanted the cheese.
8. Fox approached the tree.
9. Fox spoke to Crow.
10. Fox called her Mistress Crow.

11. Fox paid her compliments.
12. Crow looked well.
13. Crow's feathers were glossy.
14. Crow's eyes were bright.

15. Fox considered her voice superior.
16. Fox asked Crow to sing.
17. Fox would hear one song.
18. Fox would call her Queen of the Birds.

19. Crow lifted her head.
20. Crow cawed.
21. Crow opened her mouth.
22. Crow dropped the cheese.

23. Fox snapped it up.
24. Fox wanted one thing.
25. That thing was the cheese.

26. Fox gave Crow some advice.
27. "Flatterers can't be trusted."

☞ SUGGESTION: As you can see, a parable is a short story or tale that has a lesson in it. Make up your own parable with whatever moral you want to teach.

The Lake

1. Buttes surround the lake.
2. They are flat-topped.
3. They are rugged.
4. The lake is calm.
5. The lake is gray.

6. Buttes are reddish brown.
7. They are many tones.
8. They are reflected.
9. .The reflection is in the water.

10. The sky is blue.
11. The sky is mottled.
12. The weather is hot.

13. A boat comes up the lake.
14. It makes ripples in the calm.
15. The ripples shimmer.
16. It drifts slowly.
17. It nudges the beach.
18. The beach is sandy.

19. People wade ashore.
20. They are carrying tents.
21. The tents are for camping.

22. The people stand in the sand.
23. The sand is warm.
24. The sand is fine.
25. They burrow their toes.

26. They stare at the buttes.
27. They watch the colors.
28. The colors fade.
29. The colors darken.
30. A cloud shields the sun.

Morning Shower

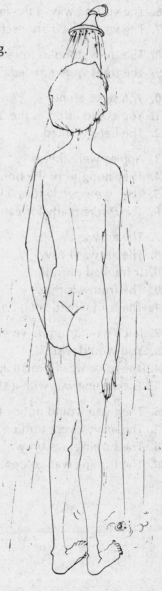

1. She was in the shower.
2. An avalanche burbled over her head.
3. The avalanche hissed.
4. It foamed down her body.
5. The foaming was in sheets.
6. The sheets were warm.

7. She relaxed under the noise.
8. She was unable to think about anything.

9. Her consciousness was focused.
10. The focusing was on the spray.
11. The spray was prickly.

12. She hummed to herself.
13. She turned slowly.
14. She turned under the showerhead.
15. The showerhead gushed.

16. The air tasted wet.
17. It tasted clean.

18. She closed her eyes.
19. Everything seemed simple.
20. The simplicity was perfect.

21. There was nothing but sensation.
22. The sensation was pure.

23. She stood that way.
24. The stand was for a long time.
25. She listened to the sound.
26. The sound was of water.
27. The water gurgled down the drain.

Orchard

1. The orchard was behind a house.
2. The house belonged to a grandfather.
3. The grandfather was mine.

4. It was a place to visit.
5. The place was a favorite.
6. The visiting was in the fall.
7. The visiting was after school.

8. The trees stood in rows.
9. The trees were gnarled.

10. You were alone.
11. You could listen to the bees.
12. The bees worked.

13. Apples were there.
14. They hung from the boughs.
15. They were ready for picking.
16. They were ready for eating.

17. The air was sweet.
18. The air was heavy.
19. It smelled of fruit.
20. The fruit was ripe.
21. The fruit would soon be rotting.

22. Juice would run down your chin.
23. You would wipe it.
24. The juice was from an apple.
25. The wiping was with a sleeve.

26. Then you would notice the leaves.
27. The leaves were turning.
28. The turning was brown.
29. The turning was golden.

☞ SUGGESTION: Maybe you can think of a "good place" that never changes in your memory. Be there again. Then write about it.

Las Vegas Light Show

1. The glitter is everywhere.
2. The neon is everywhere.

3. Enormous signs arc against the sky.
4. They bend against the sky.
5. They scoop against the sky.
6. They tower against the sky.

7. They electrify the Strip.
8. They advertise Keno.
9. They advertise twenty-one.
10. They advertise craps.
11. The advertise roulette.
12. They advertise the fun.
13. The fun is in playing slot machines.

14. The shimmer shouts a message.
15. The message is excitement.
16. The message is thrills.
17. The thrills are tawdry.
18. The message is to tourists.
19. The tourists are from out of town.

20. They come in great herds.
21. They wear sunglasses.
22. They wear hats.
23. The hats are made of straw.
24. They drift through the hotels.
25. They drift through the casinos.

26. Many are aimless.
27. Many are gawking.
28. But they spend money.
29. They hope to "beat the system."

30. The tourists keep the Light Show in operation.
31. The Light Show is dazzling.

PACE

1. Many Americans live at a pace.
2. The pace is frantic.
3. The pace is frenzied.

4. We do not have time.
5. The time is for one another.

6. Our lives sometimes have a quality.
7. The quality is strange.
8. The quality is careening.
9. This is like balls.
10. The balls smack against each other.
11. The balls are on a table.
12. The table is for billiards.

13. Handshakes are accidental.
14. They are hurried.

15. Eyes flit from place to place.
16. They avoid contact.
17. The contact would be human.

18. Talk is silly.
19. Talk is superficial.
20. Talk is rushed.

21. Leisure is something to "fill up."
22. The filling is with "fun things."

23. Vacation is a race.
24. The race is from place to place.
25. The race is high speed.

26. Work is something to be done with.
27. It is not something to do well.

28. Many institutions are run like assembly lines.
29. There is little concern for the human element.
30. There is little concern for feelings.

31. Love often seems mechanical.
32. It seems machine-stamped.
33. It seems lacking in feeling.

☞ SUGGESTION: Decide whether you agree or disagree with these generalizations about "pace" in many American lives; then write a paper describing what specific things have happened to you to support what you say. If you agree with these generalizations, you might ask yourself what's behind the pace. Beware of easy answers! If you disagree, explain why so many people think Americans live too fast.

Sunday Afternoon

1. Hank Borsini is balding.
2. He is overweight.
3. He is a little puffy under the chin.

4. But most of all he is fifty-five.
5. He has nothing to do on Sunday afternoon.

6. His kids are grown up.
7. His kids are on their own.

8. His lawn has already been fertilized.
9. It has been watered.
10. It has been mowed.
11. It has been edged.

12. He is tired of watching TV.
13. He is tired of reading.
14. The reading is of the Sunday newspaper.

15. So finally he just wanders.
16. The wandering is toward a tavern.
17. The tavern is just down the block.
18. The tavern is around the corner.

19. There the music is loud.
20. The music is brazen.

21. There the world will begin to brighten.
22. The brightening is momentary.
23. The brightening is with a beer.
24. Sometimes there are two.

25. There he can waste time.
26. The time is spent with other middle-aged men.
27. These men also have nothing to do.

☞ SUGGESTION: Describe the Sunday afternoon of some older person whom you know well. Is the situation better than Hank's or worse? Another possibility is to think about whether "personal meaning"—for you or for Hank—involves doing something useful. Is what you do who you are?

Home

1. He entered the house.
2. It was one room.
3. It was dark.
4. It smelled musty.

5. There was a hole in the ceiling.
6. Sunlight shone through the hole.
7. Dust danced on the light.

8. There was a stove.
9. The stove burned wood.
10. The stovepipe was crooked.
11. The pipe was covered with soot.

12. A cupboard stood in the corner.
13. The cupboard was old.
14. The cupboard had windows.
15. The windows were glass.
16. The glass was cracked.

17. Dishes were inside.
18. The dishes were few.
19. The dishes were mismatched.

20. There was a table.
21. The table had two leaves.
22. The table was round.
23. The table was creaky.

24. There was a bed.
25. The bed was small.
26. The bed was iron.
27. The bed had a mattress.
28. The mattress was dirty.
29. The mattress was gray.
30. The mattress was striped.

31. The floor was wooden.
32. The floor was cracked.
33. The floor was warped.
34. The warps were wavy.
35. The floor had mouse tracks.
36. The tracks were many.

37. The house was miserable.
38. The house was worthless.
39. The house was an inheritance.

40. But the house was something.
41. The house belonged to him.

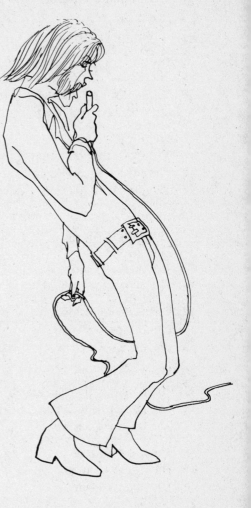

Rock Concert

1. The singer was young.
2. The singer was swarthy.
3. He stepped into the spotlight.
4. The spotlight was red.

5. His shirt was unbuttoned.
6. The unbuttoning bared his chest.

7. Sounds ballooned around him.
8. The sounds were of guitars.
9. The sounds were of drums.
10. The sounds were of girls.
11. The girls were screaming.

12. He nodded.
13. He winked.
14. The wink was to his guitarist.
15. The drummer responded with the beat.

16. The singer became animated.
17. His legs were like rubber.
18. His body jerked.
19. His head was thrown back.
20. He wailed a shout.
21. The shout was into the microphone.
22. The microphone was at his lips.

23. His movements were twisting.
24. His movements were strobed.
25. The strobing was with floodlights.

26. His voice was a garble.
27. The garble was loud.
28. The auditorium swirled.
29. The swirling was rock.
30. The rock was "heavy."

☞ NOTE: See "Model D: Multilevel Sentence" in Phase II of this book if you have trouble with sentences 16–22.

Timeless Questions

1. What is time?
2. In what sense does it "exist"?

3. These questions have worried people.
4. The worrying has been for centuries.

5. Part of the problem is a picture.
6. We have the picture.
7. The picture is in our minds.
8. The picture is of time.

9. We think of time as a line.
10. The line extends from left to right.
11. Left stands for the past.
12. The middle stands for the present.
13. Right stands for the future.

14. The picture is firmly fixed.
15. The picture is in our thinking.
16. The picture is in our way of looking.
17. Our looking is at the world.

18. The picture makes it hard to think.
19. The thinking is about time.
20. The thinking is in another way.

21. We think of the "past."
22. We think the past exists "before" the "present."

23. We think of the "present."
24. We think the present exists "before" the "future."

25. But does the "past" exist?
26. Does the "future" exist?
27. Or are they merely *ideas*?

☞ SUGGESTION: Explain your own idea about time. For instance, how long a period does "now" cover for you? Is it a moment, an hour, a day, a week? Does your idea of "now" depend on what you are doing and what you are thinking about?

Fish Story

1. The pole quivered.
2. The pole was for fishing.
3. The pole was slim.
4. The pole seemed alive.
5. The line tightened.
6. The bobber dipped into the water.

7. The reel ticked.
8. The line unwound.
9. The line was clear.
10. The line was nylon.

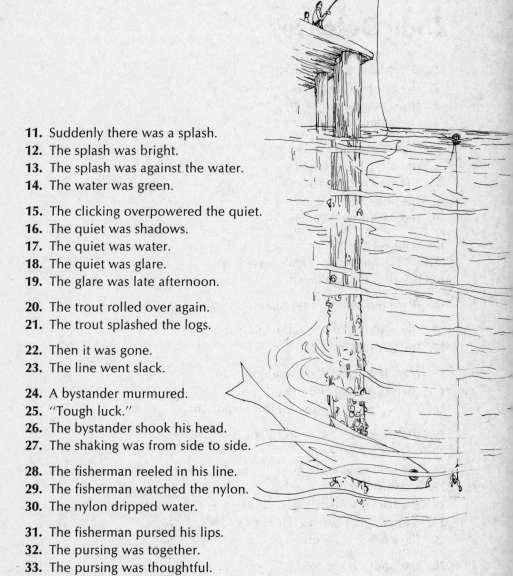

11. Suddenly there was a splash.
12. The splash was bright.
13. The splash was against the water.
14. The water was green.

15. The clicking overpowered the quiet.
16. The quiet was shadows.
17. The quiet was water.
18. The quiet was glare.
19. The glare was late afternoon.

20. The trout rolled over again.
21. The trout splashed the logs.

22. Then it was gone.
23. The line went slack.

24. A bystander murmured.
25. "Tough luck."
26. The bystander shook his head.
27. The shaking was from side to side.

28. The fisherman reeled in his line.
29. The fisherman watched the nylon.
30. The nylon dripped water.

31. The fisherman pursed his lips.
32. The pursing was together.
33. The pursing was thoughtful.

34. The fisherman grinned.
35. "That's okay."
36. The fisherman wrinkled his nose.
37. "I fish for the halibut."

Body Defenses

1. Our health is safeguarded.
2. The safeguarding is by defenses.
3. The defenses are a series.
4. The series is remarkable.

5. These defenses are like an army
6. The army is ready.
7. It forms chemical lines.
8. The lines are in succession.
9. They ward off invaders.

10. Suppose an example.
11. Suppose some dust gets in your eye.
12. The dust is germ laden.

13. There is probably nothing to worry about.

14. The eye's surface is bathed in tears.
15. The bathing is quick.

16. Tears help wash away the dust.
17. They also serve another purpose.
18. This purpose is perhaps more important.

19. The tears contain an antiseptic.
20. It is called lysozyme.
21. It is very powerful.
22. It destroys most bacteria.
23. The bacteria might be harmful.
24. Harm might come to the eye's surface.
25. The surface is delicate.

26. The body "overprotects" itself.
27. Overprotection is for self-defense.
28. Overprotection is for survival.

29. Lysozyme is a case in point.
30. It dramatizes this idea.

31. Teardrops can be diluted.
32. The dilution is with a half-gallon of water.
33. Lysozyme will still destroy germs.
34. The germs are dangerous.
35. Their danger is potential.

Automatic Sharpener

1. He gripped the two ears.
2. They were chromed.
3. They were on top of the sharpener.
4. The sharpener was new.
5. The sharpener was self-feeding.

6. He pressed them together.
7. The pressing was between his thumb.
8. The pressing was between his forefinger.

9. The grippers were spring-loaded.
10. The grippers opened in an "O."
11. The "O" was small.
12. The "O" was like lips about to whistle.

13. He pushed the pencil in.
14. He slid the yoke.
15. The yoke was for clamping.
16. The yoke went up the pencil.
17. The pencil was new.
18. The pencil was yellow.

19. He watched the grippers.
20. They dug in.
21. The machinery was set.

22. He turned the handle.
23. The turning was slow.
24. The turning was forward.
25. The turning was in circles.
26. He felt the tip.
27. The tip was blunt.
28. It ground away.
29. The grinding was under a press.
30. The press was made of edges.
31. The edges were for cutting.

32. He squeezed the ears together.
33. He let the vise snap.
34. It snapped against the sharpener.

35. The pencil had a tip.
36. It was black.
37. It was pointed.
38. The point was clean.

39. It was a cone.
40. The cone was perfect.
41. The cone was graphite.
42. The cone was above a row.
43. The row was of teeth marks.
44. The teeth marks were mechanical.

☞ SUGGESTION: Spend a few minutes with something you can do over and over—like playing a pinball machine, ironing a shirt, getting into and out of an easy chair, sweeping the floor, lighting a cigarette. Any simple, repeated, mechanical process is fair game. Pay attention to each part of the process, then write about it so that the reader can share the experience.

High Noon

1. Tex steps into the dust.
2. The dust is ankle deep.
3. The dust is on Main Street.
4. Main Street is in Dodge City.

5. The sun booms down.
6. The booming is like a hammer.
7. The hammer is heavy.

8. Tex is tense.
9. Tex is waiting.

10. Sweat rolls down.
11. Sweat rolls from the band.
12. The band is on his hat.
13. The hat is high-peaked.

14. The Stranger is down the street.
15. The Stranger is striding.
16. The stride is toward Tex.

17. Tex blinks at the sweat.
18. Tex wishes he hadn't worn the hat.
19. The hat is heavy.
20. The hat is sweltering.

21. The Stranger looks mean.
22. The Stranger is dressed in black.

23. Tex swallows the dryness.
24. The dryness is in his throat.
25. Tex squints.
26. The squinting is fierce.
27. Tex hopes to slow down the Stranger.

28. The Stranger pauses.
29. His face is shadowed.
30. The shadowing is beneath his hat.
31. The hat is black.

32. "Draw!"
33. The Stranger shouts.

34. But Tex holds his ground.
35. Tex is trembling.
36. Tex is in the sun.
37. The sun is sizzling.

38. People are watching.
39. They watch from storefronts.
40. The people are curious.

41. "I'd prefer not to."
42. Tex whispers.
43. The whisper is husky.

44. The Stranger looks stunned.
45. "What?"
46. The Stranger asks.

47. "I work the graveyard shift."
48. Tex answers.
49. "I'm not on duty."

50. The Stranger's face darkens.
51. Rage darkens his face.

52. The Stranger speaks.
53. "I traveled fifty miles.
54. This is a showdown."

55. Sweat pours.
56. The pouring is down Tex's back.
57. The pouring is from under his arms.

58. He has forgotten his deodorant.
59. The deodorant is a spray.

60. He begins to feel embarrassed.
61. He is embarrassed about his odor.

62. "I'm sorry."
63. Tex mumbles.
64. "The marshal is out of town."

65. "Then you're going to die."
66. The Stranger speaks.
67. His tone is venomous.

68. Tex feels a rock.
69. The rock is in his shoe.
70. The rock is next to his toe.

71. "But I'm a *pacifist*."
72. Tex cries out.
73. The cry is a shout.
74. The shout is loud.

75. "A *what*?"
76. The Stranger barks.

77. "You heard me."
78. Tex speaks.
79. He speaks with a wink.
80. The wink is friendly.
81. "I don't believe in violence."

82. The Stranger shakes his head.
83. The Stranger is confused.

84. "Try it."
85. Tex adds.
86. "You'll like it."

☞ SUGGESTION: Finish "High Noon."

MODEL

1. She is only fifteen years old.
2. She is a model.
3. She is famous.

4. She has learned her trade well.
5. The trade is selling fashions.

6. She is a picture.
7. The picture is of fashion.
8. The picture is from head to toe.
9. Her skin is natural.
10. It is healthy.
11. It is like a blush.
12. The blush is pink.

13. Her eyes are accented.
14. The accent is eye shadow.
15. The accent is mascara.

16. Her lips are natural.
17. Her lips are tinted only with lip gloss.

18. Her hair is long.
19. The length is fashionable.
20. Her hair is blond.
21. Her hair is straight.
22. Her hair is pulled back from her face.

23. Her dress is blue.
24. The blue is like cobalt.
25. The collar is long.
26. The dress is accented by a scarf.
27. The scarf is reddish orange.
28. The dress is short.
29. The dress is pleated.

30. Her stockings are the "wet look."
31. Her stockings are blue.
32. The blue is darker.
33. The blue complements the dress.

34. Her shoes also match the dress.
35. Her shoes have square toes.
36. The heels are wide.
37. Buckles are on the shoes.

38. The model wears rings.
39. The rings are on her fingers.
40. She wears a watch.
41. The watch is large.
42. The watch has a red band.

43. She likes fashion.
44. She looks great.

☞ NOTE: Do you like the last two sentences better separate or combined? Why?

laser

1. The laser beam is light.
2. The light is a special kind.
3. The light is intense.
4. It differs from ordinary light.

5. Ordinary light has many colors.
6. Its waves move.
7. The movement is random.
8. The movement is in many directions.

9. Laser light is monochromatic.
10. Its waves move.
11. The movement is in a single direction.

12. Photons in ordinary light spread out.
13. They diffuse their energy.
14. Laser beam photons are concentrated.
15. They focus their energy.

16. The beam is generated by a device.
17. The beam is amplified by a device.
18. The device is called a laser.
19. The device emits light waves.
20. The light waves are spaced.
21. The light waves are parallel.

22. The beam has characteristics.
23. The characteristics are unique.
24. The characteristics can lead to applications.
25. The applications can be peaceful.
26. The applications can be destructive.

27. A laser can be focused.
28. It can be transmitted.
29. It can heat a TV dinner.
30. The dinner can be a thousand miles away.

31. But a laser could be focused on a tank.
32. It could be focused on a ship.
33. It could be focused on an aircraft.
34. It could burn a hole.
35. The burning would be almost instantaneous.
36. The burning would be through armor.
37. The armor would be metal.

38. A laser beam can be used to weld retinas.
39. The retinas have loosened from the eye.
40. The welding does not destroy the tissue.

41. But a laser could be used to destroy.
42. Human life would be destroyed.
43. The destruction would be in a flash.

44. A laser beam can be used to carry signals.
45. The signals are for radio.
46. The signals are for television.
47. The signals are for communications.
48. The communications are by telephone.

49. But a laser could also be used from space.
50. The use would be as a ray.
51. The ray would cause death.
52. The death would be to enemies.

53. Thus laser light is not ordinary.
54. Its uses are not ordinary.

☞ SUGGESTION: This brief essay explains laser beams by showing point by point how they differ from ordinary light. First the writer tells something about laser light, then something about ordinary light. Notice, too, that the peaceful and destructive applications of lasers are developed by using the same basic method. Write a short paper of your own, explaining something you are familiar with in terms of something your readers probably already understand. Follow the same general pattern used in the laser essay—a step-by-step comparison of two things.

Sailor's Home

1. The sailor sails the ship.
2. He stands behind the wheel.

3. His shoulders are broad.
4. His arms are muscular.
5. His mouth is open.

6. His teeth are yellow.
7. Some are broken.
8. Some are missing.

9. His lips are thick.
10. His lips are chapped.
11. His lips are rough.
12. Years have toughened his lips.
13. The years were spent at sea.

14. His hands are on the wheel.
15. His hands are large.
16. His hands are strong.
17. His hands can feel.
18. His hands feel movement.
19. The movement is the ship's.
20. His hands control the movement.

21. His ship is large.
22. His ship has sails.
23. The sails are white.
24. The sails are canvas.
25. The sails catch the breeze.
26. The sails billow in the breeze.

27. The sailor is going home.
28. Home is in Halifax.
29. His family is in Halifax.
30. His family is waiting.

31. It has been a time.
32. The time has been long.
33. The time has been spent on the sea.

34. The sailor thinks of home.
35. His house is large.
36. His house is made of stone.
37. His house has a bay window.
38. His house stands on a hill.
39. His house is surrounded by grass.
40. The grass is always green.
41. The green reminds him.
42. The reminder is of the sea.

43. The sailor looks to the shore.
44. The sailor looks to his hill.
45. The shore is coming into view.
46. The hill is coming into view.

47. He is coming home.

Television

1. Television can help us see.
2. We see the pattern.
3. The pattern is life.
4. The life is in America.

5. Television can help us to understand.
6. We understand events.
7. The events unite us.
8. The events divide us.

9. Consider an example.
10. The example is death.
11. The death was of leaders.
12. The leaders were political.
13. The leaders included John Kennedy.
14. The leaders included Martin Luther King, Jr.
15. The leaders included Robert Kennedy.

16. These deaths united the nation.
17. The unification was profound.

18. Grief became an experience.
19. Shame became an experience.
20. The experience was shared.
21. The whole nation shared.

22. Television let us participate.
23. The participation was intense.
24. The participation was dramatic.
25. The participation was in events.
26. The events were historical.

27. We were joined.
28. The joining was with other people.
29. The joining was for a few moments.
30. The moments were electric.

31. An event happened.
32. The event was similar.
33. The event was in 1969.
34. The event was the landing.
35. The landing was on the moon.
36. The event was the walk.
37. The walk was man's.
38. The walk was first.
39. The walk was on the moon.

40. Here the occasion was joyful.
41. The occasion was exciting.
42. The occasion was a "step."
43. The step was for mankind.
44. The step was giant.

45. But television can also divide us.
46. The dividing is from each other.

47. The dividing has occurred in confrontations.
48. Confrontations were between young and old.
49. Confrontations were betweeen radicals and conservatives.
50. Confrontations were between police and students.
51. Confrontations were between blacks and whites.
52. Confrontations were between hawks and doves.

53. The confrontations have dramatized feelings.
54. The feelings are beneath the surface.
55. Society has a surface.

56. The confrontations have shown Americans.
57. The Americans are in conflicts.
58. The conflicts stem from our policy.
59. The policy is in Southeast Asia.
60. The conflicts range to busing.
61. The busing is of school children.

62. Such events have provided an opportunity.
63. The events are spectacular.
64. The opportunity is for bigots.
65. The bigots promote thinking.
66. The thinking is stereotyped.

67. These confrontations have infected our wounds.
68. The wounds are social.
69. The wounds are emotional.

70. So television does more than transmit.
71. The transmission is of movies.
72. The transmission is of weather.
73. The transmission is of variety shows.
74. The transmission is of sports.

75. Television helps shape our feelings.
76. The feelings are toward each other.
77. The feelings are toward ourselves.
78. Television sometimes unites us.
79. Television sometimes divides us.

☞ NOTE: Sentences 1–4 and 5–8 of "Television" represent the thesis, or main idea, of this essay. Sentences 75–79 conclude the essay by repeating this main idea.

Truck Stop

1. The drivers line up.
2. The drivers drive trucks.
3. The line is along the counter.
4. The counter is grease-smudged.

5. The drivers sip their coffee.
6. The coffee is strong.
7. The coffee is bitter.
8. The drivers watch a waitress.
9. The waitress is young.
10. The waitress walks to the kitchen.
11. The waitress walks to the counter.

12. The waitress is smiling.
13. The waitress is friendly.
14. Her friendliness is teasing.
15. The waitress is slender.
16. The waitress is pretty.

17. Outside are sounds.
18. Traffic makes the sounds.
19. The sounds are of morning.

20. Inside are sounds.
21. Men make the sounds.
22. The men are hard working.
23. The men laugh.
24. The sounds are lusty.
25. The sounds are cheerful.

26. The waitress pours coffee.
27. The waitress serves doughnuts.
28. The waitress serves pies.
29. The waitress grins at each driver.
30. The grin is innocent.
31. The innocence is adolescent.

32. Some drivers try to amuse the waitress.
33. The try is with remarks.
34. The remarks are coarse.
35. The remarks are suggestive.

36. The waitress blushes.
37. The waitress winks.
38. The waitress pours more coffee.

39. One driver flexes his arms.
40. The driver tightens his shoulders.
41. The flexing is for her benefit.
42. The tightening is for her benefit.

43. One by one the drivers pay their bills.
44. The drivers leave tips.
45. The tips are bigger than usual.

Operation Breadbasket

1. Operation Breadbasket is a project.
2. The project is intended to bring pressure.
3. The pressure is on businesses.
4. The businesses are white.
5. The businesses often discriminate.
6. The discrimination is against blacks.

7. The operation has been organized.
8. The organizers are leaders.
9. The leaders are in the black community.

10. Its aim is to improve conditions.
11. The conditions are economic.
12. The conditions have oppressed blacks.
13. The conditions have oppressed for years.

14. Its tool is the boycott.
15. The tool is most effective.
16. The tool is used.
17. Its use is widespread.

18. (A boycott is a refusal.
19. The refusal is by a group.
20. The refusal is to patronize a business.
21. The business is unfair.
22. The unfairness is to the group.)

23. Sometimes the business is a store.
24. The group does not buy there.
25. The group urges its friends.
26. The urging is not to buy there.
27. The store loses money.

28. Sometimes the business manufactures things.
29. The things are sold to stores.

30. Scrubbo Company makes soap.
31. Scrubbo Company does not hire blacks.
32. The soap is sold in many stores.

33. The group does not buy Scrubbo.
34. The group tells the storeowners.
35. "Blacks won't buy Scrubbo.
36. Scrubbo Company does not hire Negroes."

37. The storeowners complain to Scrubbo Company.
38. The storeowners stop stocking Scrubbo.
39. Scrubbo Company loses money.

40. Operation Breadbasket has aims.
41. The aims are specific.
42. The aims are long range.

43. The project has hopes.
44. The hopes are to increase the jobs.
45. The jobs are for blacks.
46. The hopes are to increase the sales.
47. The sales are of products.
48. The products are made by blacks.

49. And it has already gotten results.
50. The results are impressive.
51. The results are by means.
52. The means are nonviolent.

53. It has helped numbers of blacks.
54. The numbers are large.
55. The help is to get jobs.
56. The jobs were "not available" before.

57. It has helped products.
58. The products are many.
59. The products are black.
60. The products are to be sold.
61. The selling is in stores.
62. The stores did not carry the products before.

63. It has helped blacks to work.
64. The working is together.
65. The working is for survival.
66. The survival is their own.
67. The survival is in business.

68. Operation Breadbasket has been a project.
69. Operation Breadbasket has been successful.

☞ SUGGESTION: Have you ever worked with a group that was trying to change something the group thought was unfair—something at school, in your neighborhood, or in your town? If you have, write a paper explaining what the problem was, what the group did, and what the results were.

Public Library

1. It was morning.
2. It was Saturday.
3. It was warm.
4. It was spring.
5. It was clear.

6. A few people waited on the steps.
7. The steps were to the library.
8. The steps were stone.
9. Some watched the cars.
10. Some watched the buses.
11. The cars rolled by.
12. The buses rolled by.

13. A man sat on a bench.
14. The man was old.
15. The man held his hat.
16. The man crossed his legs.
17. The man uncrossed his legs.
18. The man was dressed in gray.
19. The gray was faded.

20. Two people slouched.
21. The people were young.
22. The people slouched against the building.
23. The people were relaxed.

24. There was almost no talk.

25. A woman closed her eyes.
26. The woman was fat.
27. The woman soaked in the sun.
28. The sun was warm.

29. Most people watched the street.
30. Most people squinted.
31. Most people yawned.

32. Their faces were still.
33. The stillness was from thought.
34. Or the stillness was from boredom.

35. They did not talk about books.
36. They did not talk about ideas.
37. They did not talk about why they were there.
38. They did not talk about what they hoped to learn.

39. Everybody waited.
40. The waiting was for the chiming.
41. The chiming was at 9:00 A.M.
42. The chiming signaled the opening.
43. The opening was of the doors.
44. The doors were to the library.
45. The opening was to a world.
46. The world was of print.

☞ SUGGESTION: Describe a group of people who are waiting for something—for example, students waiting for a class, people waiting for a bus, shoppers waiting for a store to open. Try to limit the size of the group to five or ten people.

Hydrogen Bomb

1. A hydrogen bomb is a series.
2. The series is made up of bombs.

3. Some bombs trigger a sequence.
4. The bombs that trigger are smaller.
5. The sequence is reactions.
6. The reactions result in an explosion.
7. The reaction is called "fission."
8. The fission is thermonuclear.

9. The sequence begins.
10. The beginning is a detonation.
11. The detonation is of TNT.
12. TNT compresses U-235.

13. The sequence causes fission.
14. Fission releases neutrons.

15. The temperature rises.
16. The rise is of millions of degrees.
17. The degrees are on the Celsius Scale.

18. The neutrons strike nuclei.
19. The nuclei are lithium.
20. The striking transforms nuclei.
21. The transformation is into helium.
22. The transformation is into tritium.

23. The tritium fuses with deuterium.
24. This fusion produces more neutrons.
25. The neutrons strike the casing.
26. The casing is U-238.

27. This fusion produces a second stage.
28. The stage is fission.
29. The fission causes a release.
30. The release is enormous.
31. The release is of energy.

32. The release causes an explosion.
33. The explosion has a range.
34. The range is greater than that of the A-bomb.
35. The range is ten times greater.

36. The H-bomb has a "blast effect."
37. The effect extends over ten miles.
38. The effect is destruction.
39. Buildings are destroyed.
40. The destruction is total.
41. Or the destruction is partial.
42. Destruction depends on nearness.
43. The nearness is to the blast.

44. The H-bomb has a "flash effect."
45. The effect extends over twenty miles.
46. The effect is burning.
47. People are burned.

☞ NOTE: In "Hydrogen Bomb," there are several opportunities for combining groups of sentences. Look for the word in each group that links the group to earlier sentences. Read your sentences aloud and explore the options.

DAWN

1. The night had been brittle cold.
2. It had been black.
3. It had been pierced.
4. Slivers pierced the night.
5. The slivers were light.
6. The slivers were from the city.

7. Trains rumbled in the switchyard.
8. Trains moved the freight.
9. The moving was down rails.
10. The rails were steel.
11. The rails glittered.

12. A siren wailed in the distance.
13. The sound rose.
14. The sound fell.
15. The sound trailed off.
16. The trail was into silence.
17. The silence was empty.

18. Taxicabs rolled down streets.
19. The streets were bare.
20. The streets were deserted.
21. The desertion seemed ominous.
22. The taxicabs fanned the buildings.
23. The fanning was with their headlights.

24. The blackness began to soften.
25. The blackness was in the east.
26. The softening was steady.
27. The softening was into a gray.
28. The gray was deep.
29. The gray was charcoal.

30. The sky lightened further.
31. The sky revealed outlines.
32. The outlines were of buildings.
33. The buildings were black.
34. The buildings were against the horizon.

35. Gray then warmed into grayish rose.
36. The grayish rose was soft.

37. A layer of clouds was backlighted.
38. The backlighting was by dawn.
39. Dawn worked its way.
40. The working was across the horizon.

41. "Incredible!"
42. The director chuckled.
43. The director smiled.
44. The smile stretched from ear to ear.

45. The cameraman frowned.
46. The cameraman narrowed his eyes.
47. The cameraman spoke.
48. "Uh, I think I forgot to load the film."

How Whites Look to Blacks

1. Leaders have been critical.
2. The criticism has been for years.
3. The leaders are in a community.
4. The community is black.
5. The criticism is of stereotypes.
6. The stereotypes are held by whites.

7. But a poll reveals something.
8. The poll is recent.
9. Blacks also have stereotypes.
10. The stereotypes are racial.
11. The stereotypes are of whites.

12. The poll revealed statistics.
13. The statistics suggest something.
14. The something concerns a perspective.
15. The perspective is black.
16. The perspective is in America today.

17. Seventy-seven percent of blacks agreed.
18. Their agreement was with a proposition.
19. This proposition was that whites are repressive.
20. The repression is deliberate.

21. Seventy-four percent had a feeling.
22. The feeling was that whites want women.
23. The women are black.

24. About two-thirds had an agreement.
25. The agreement was that whites are mean.
26. This meanness is basic.
27. The agreement was that whites are selfish.
28. This selfishness is basic.

29. Over half regarded whites as weaker than blacks.
30. The weakness is physical.

31. Sixty-three percent of the blacks feel something.
32. The something is that whites are regretful.
33. Their regret is for having abolished slavery.

34. Two-thirds feel that whites are scared.
35. Their fear is that blacks are better people than they are.

36. Eighty percent are in agreement.
37. This percentage is whopping.
38. The agreement is that whites consider blacks inferior.

39. These statistics are interesting to whites.
40. The statistics express feelings.
41. The feelings have been repressed too long.
42. The repression has been within the community.
43. The community is black.

44. Maybe blacks can understand their prejudices.
45. Maybe whites can understand their prejudices.
46. The understanding is by looking.
47. The looking is through each other's eyes.

Dropout

1. She sleeps in.
2. She sleeps till ten o'clock.
3. She sleeps every day of the week.
4. Then she gets up.
5. She yawns.
6. She looks out the window.

7. The world moves by.
8. The moving is with a hum.
9. The hum is purposeful.

10. Her face is red.
11. Her face is blotchy.
12. The blotchiness is from the night before.

13. She is surprised at herself.
14. Now she does anything for a laugh.
15. Now she does anything for relief.
16. The relief is for a moment.
17. The relief is from boredom.
18. The boredom is daily.

19. She puts on her bathrobe.
20. She ties the sash.
21. The sash is pink.
22. The sash is white.
23. Her waist is beginning to bulge.
24. The bulge is slight.

25. She pads into the kitchen.
26. She looks for something.
27. She wants to eat.

28. The dishes are stacked.
29. The dishes are dirty.
30. The stacking is from the night before.
31. The stacking is in the sink.
32. The stacking is on the drainboard.

33. She flicks on the radio.
34. The flicking is with a turn.
35. The turn is irritated.
36. The turn is impatient.

37. Music throbs through the tubes.
38. The music is country style.
39. The music fills the room.
40. The filling is with sounds.
41. The sounds are of days.
42. The days are similar.

43. She finds some cereal.
44. She finds some milk.
45. She fixes her breakfast.
46. She listens to the radio.

47. The day stretches before her.
48. The day is like a desert.
49. The desert is treeless.

50. She wonders what to do.

51. The dishes are dirty.
52. The ironing needs to be done.
53. The floor needs dusting.
54. She is too tired.

55. She would like to go shopping.
56. Clothes are expensive.
57. Clothes would be new.

58. She thinks about her friends.
59. The friends are in school.
60. The friends are sitting through their classes.
61. The classes are boring.
62. The friends are waiting for lunch.

63. It is fun.
64. The fun is to be out of school.

65. School was a drag.
66. School was a waste.
67. The waste was her time.
68. Her time was valuable.

69. She walks into the living room.
70. She turns on the TV.
71. She sits down.
72. She watches the soap operas.

73. She can almost hear herself talking.
74. The talking will be later tonight.
75. The talking will be to someone.
76. Someone will ask her something.
77. The something is about being out of school.

78. "Groovy," she will say.
79. "Really a gas."

☞ SUGGESTION: If you have been out of school, because of illness or because you dropped out or for some other reason, write a paper telling how you spent your time. If you found it pleasant or unpleasant, tell why. If you have never missed any school, explain why.

Schools and Free Enterprise

1. The people are few.
2. The people are asking a question.
3. The question is about schools.
4. The question is about management.
5. The management is of education.

6. The question is simple.
7. The question is unsettling.
8. The unsettling is profound.
9. The question is unsettling to teachers.
10. The question is unsettling to administrators.

11. Why not make schools compete?
12. The competition would be for customers.

13. These people make a comparison.
14. The comparison is with business.
15. The comparison is with schools.

16. Business operates under a system.
17. The system is free enterprise.
18. The system causes business to improve.
19. The improvement is in efficiency.

20. Business struggles.
21. The struggle is for customers.
22. Business works hard.
23. The work is to increase production.
24. The work is to increase services.
25. The work is to attract customers.

26. Survival is based on ability.
27. The ability is to compete.
28. The competition succeeds.

29. These people propose experiments.
30. The experiments would stimulate competition.
31. The competition would be among schools.
32. The competition would be among teachers.
33. The competition would be to get students.

34. Each child would have an allowance.
35. The allowance would be to pay.
36. The payment would be for education.
37. The allowance could be spent at any school.

38. The selection would be made by parents.
39. The selection would be of schools.
40. The parents would examine the courses.
41. The courses would be taught at the schools.
42. The parents would examine the teachers.
43. The teachers would be employed by the schools.
44. The parents would examine the other students.
45. The other students would be enrolled in the schools.

46. The parents would look at the system.
47. The system would be testing.
48. The system would be grading.
49. The system would be discipline.

50. The parents would decide.
51. The decision would be whether they approved.
52. The approval would be of the system.
53. The system would be used in the school.

54. Some schools would not please parents.
55. These schools would lose students.
56. These schools would lose money.
57. These schools would shut down.

58. Parents would be the experts.
59. The experts would be in education.
60. Parents would decide.
61. The decision would be what to teach.
62. The decision would be how to teach it.

63. Parents would read the advertisements.
64. The advertisements would make claims.
65. The claims would be about accomplishments.
66. The accomplishments would be made by the schools.
67. Some claims would be exaggerated.
68. A few claims would be accurate.

69. But the system would be competitive.

Motorcycle Pack

1. We could hear them coming.
2. They were way off in the distance.
3. They were winding down the road.
4. The road was through the mountains.
5. The road was east of town.

6. The sound made us think of power saws.
7. But the sound was more sustained.
8. The sound was deeper.
9. The sound got louder.

10. The first one broke into view.
11. He was at the edge of town.
12. The edge is where the brush is thick.
13. The brush was full of shadows.

14. The others swarmed behind him.
15. The others rapped their pipes.
16. The others brought the noise.
17. The noise was like a wave.

18. The leader geared down.
19. The gearing down was at the grocery store.
20. The leader set the pace.
21. The pace was swaggering.
22. The pace was through the middle of town.

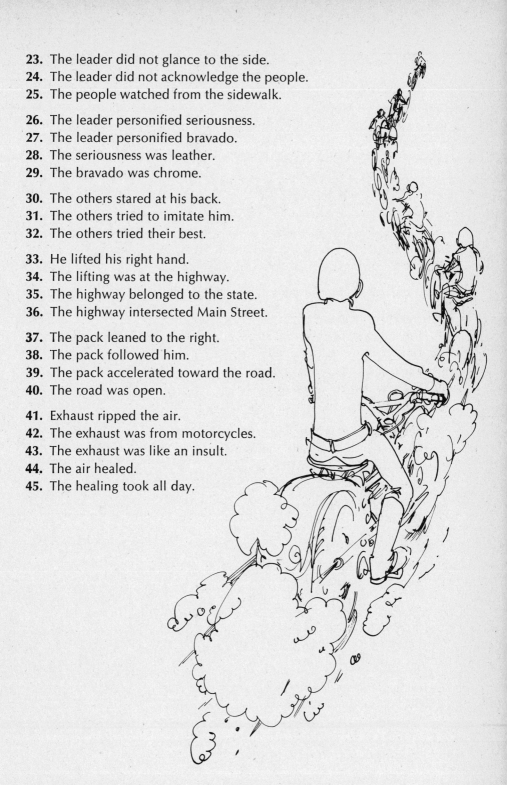

23. The leader did not glance to the side.
24. The leader did not acknowledge the people.
25. The people watched from the sidewalk.

26. The leader personified seriousness.
27. The leader personified bravado.
28. The seriousness was leather.
29. The bravado was chrome.

30. The others stared at his back.
31. The others tried to imitate him.
32. The others tried their best.

33. He lifted his right hand.
34. The lifting was at the highway.
35. The highway belonged to the state.
36. The highway intersected Main Street.

37. The pack leaned to the right.
38. The pack followed him.
39. The pack accelerated toward the road.
40. The road was open.

41. Exhaust ripped the air.
42. The exhaust was from motorcycles.
43. The exhaust was like an insult.
44. The air healed.
45. The healing took all day.

Slave Keepers

1. Some species keep slaves.
2. The species are ants.
3. The purpose is survival.

4. The amazon ant is best known for this practice.

5. The amazon is large.
6. The amazon is brownish red.
7. The amazon is widespread.
8. The spreading is over regions.
9. The regions are temperate.
10. The regions are in North America.

11. The amazons assemble.
12. The assembly is outside their nest.
13. Then they begin to march.
14. The march is toward a colony.
15. The colony is of ants.
16. The ants are black.
17. The colony is to be raided.

18. A battle takes place.
19. The battle is around the nest.
20. The nest belongs to the victims.
21. The victims are unlucky.

22. The amazons use their jaws.
23. The jaws are sharp.
24. The jaws are sickle-shaped.
25. The jaws pierce heads.
26. The jaws pierce bodies.
27. The heads belong to the black ants.
28. The bodies belong to the black ants.

29. The black ants gnaw at the legs.
30. The legs belong to the attackers.
31. The gnawing is in defense.
32. The defense is hopeless.

33. Then the amazons seize the pupae.
34. The pupae are the offspring.
35. The offspring are developing.
36. The offspring are of the black ants.
37. The amazons carry the offspring away.
38. The carrying is back to the nest.
39. The nest belongs to the amazons.
40. The amazons leave the black ants behind.
41. The black ants are dead.

42. The pupae develop into black ants.
43. The pupae develop in captivity.

44. The pupae spend their lives working.
45. The work is for the amazons.
46. The work is finding food.
47. The food is to feed their captors.

48. The amazons are dependent.
49. The dependence is on their slaves.
50. The jaws are useless.
51. The jaws belong to the amazons.
52. The uselessness is for finding food.
53. The uselessness is for digging.
54. The uselessness is for feeding themselves.

55. The amazons have become specialized.
56. Their specialty is fighting.
57. Now they are enslaved to their slaves.
58. They cannot survive without them.

Commune

1. Their life seems simple.
2. Their life seems idyllic.
3. This appearance is to outsiders.

4. Their dress seems eccentric.
5. It ranges from Indian robes.
6. It ranges to work clothes.
7. It ranges to mod gear.

8. Their talk seems to be a code.
9. The talk is stylized.
10. The code identifies insiders.
11. The code excludes outsiders.

12. They are the People's Commune.
13. They are a group.
14. The group is organized for support.
15. The support is mutual.

16. Their critics accuse them.
17. The accusation is of wasting time.

18. They criticize the critics.
19. The criticism is for not taking time.
20. Time is for enjoying life.

21. They come.
22. They go.
23. They vary in their sincerity.
24. They vary in their maturity.

25. Sometimes they lounge.
26. The lounging is on the porch.
27. They soak up the sun.
28. They talk to each other.
29. Their talk is about love.
30. Their talk is about music.
31. Their talk is about war.
32. Their talk is about peace.

33. Sometimes they watch the tourists.
34. The tourists have come to see them.

35. And sometimes they rap.
36. The rap is with the tourists.
37. The tourists feel amusement.
38. The tourists feel curiosity.
39. The tourists feel hostility.
40. The tourists feel embarrassment.
41. The tourists don't feel indifference.

42. Their life has had an effect.
43. The effect is long range.
44. The effect is on the tourists.
45. The effect is on the observers.
46. The observers gawk.

47. Many have been shocked.
48. The shock is into an awareness.
49. The awareness is new.
50. The awareness is of possibilities.
51. The possibilities would be for existence.
52. The existence would be an alternative.
53. The possibilities would be different.
54. The difference would be from suburbia.

55. A few have learned something.
56. They learned from the contrast.
57. The contrast is in styles.
58. The styles are in living.

☞ SUGGESTION: What can people learn from talking with commune "families"? If it is possible to learn from communes, why are so many people outraged or shocked by them?

The Hopi Way

1. The Hopi Indians are a tribe.
2. The tribe is remarkable.
3. The tribe lives on a reservation.
4. The reservation is in the mountains.
5. The reservation is in the desert.
6. The reservation is in Arizona.

7. The word "Hopi" can be translated.
8. The translation is "peaceful."
9. The translation is "happy."
10. This description is appropriate.
11. The description is for a culture.
12. The culture lacks tenseness.
13. The culture lacks competition.
14. The culture lacks materialism.

15. The Hopi are like other tribes.
16. The tribes are in North America.
17. The Hopi have a sense.
18. The sense is strong.
19. The sense is of "extended family."
20. "Extended family" means attachment.
21. The attachment is to other Hopi.
22. The attachment is to their heritage.
23. The attachment is to ceremonies.

24. But the Hopi are unlike other tribes.
25. The other tribes include the Navajo.
26. The Navajo are more aggressive.
27. The Navajo are widely dispersed.
28. The dispersion is over a reservation.
29. The Navajo reservation surrounds the Hopi.

30. The family teaches the Hopi.
31. He is taught "The Hopi Way."
32. "The Hopi Way" is a system.
33. The system is values.
34. The system is behavior.
35. The system runs deep.
36. The system runs through the culture.

37. The society is "matriarchal."
38. The mother represents authority.
39. The mother represents lineage.
40. "Lineage" means "line of descent."

41. Families belong to clans.
42. The clans extend over a territory.
43. The territory is wide.
44. The clans create a network.
45. The network is intricate.
46. The network is associations.
47. The network is relationships.

48. The customs concern kinship.
49. The customs are tribal.
50. The customs forbid in-clan marriage.

51. The chief is a counselor.
52. The chief is for the village.
53. The chief helps the people.
54. The help is to follow precepts.
55. The precepts are ancient.
56. The precepts are Hopi.
57. The chief does not issue orders.
58. The chief does not possess power.

59. The Hopi learn self-discipline.
60. The Hopi learn restraint.
61. The Hopi learn concern.
62. The concern is for welfare.
63. The welfare is of members.
64. The "extended family" has members.
65. The learning is at an early age.

66. Children share responsibilities.
67. The responsibilities are economic.
68. The responsibilities are to the family.
69. They learn to work.

70. They work without urging.
71. Work is part of their obligation.
72. Work is worthwhile in itself.
73. Work is not to be dreaded.
74. Work is not done for rewards.

75. The Hopi learn to believe.
76. The belief is in continuity.
77. Continuity is in the universe.
78. The belief is in forces.
79. The forces are spiritual.
80. The forces manifest themselves.
81. The manifesting is through reality.
82. The reality is physical.

83. They view things.
84. They see processes.
85. The processes are dynamic.
86. They try to remain in harmony.
87. Their harmony is with the universe.

88. Their prayer is an exercise.
89. The exercise is will.
90. The exercise is not supplication.
91. They have a belief.
92. Human beings cause change.
93. Change is caused by an act.
94. The act is from will.
95. The will is individual.
96. Or the will is collective.

97. Every Hopi is responsible.
98. The responsibility is to direct thoughts.
99. The responsibility is to direct desires.
100. The direction is "The Hopi Way."
101. "The Hopi Way" is toward the constructive.
102. "The Hopi Way" is toward the good.
103. "The Hopi Way" is away from the destructive.
104. "The Hopi Way" is away from evil.

105. Thoughts must be turned.
106. The turning is toward health.
107. The turning is toward strength.
108. The turning is toward happiness.
109. These represent "The Hopi Way."
110. It is the way of harmony.

☞ SUGGESTION: (1) Imagine yourself as a Hopi Indian who is suddenly transported into the neighborhood where you live; try to see things as you think he might, using an "I" point of view. Or (2) use any of the points about Hopi life developed above as a "springboard" for a comparison or contrast with *your* culture. Or (3) comment on whether "The Hopi Way" is practical for American culture or for your own personal philosophy.

Drag Racer

1. The sun was blistering.
2. The blistering was hot.

3. The sand glittered.
4. The gravel glittered.
5. They reflected the heat.
6. The heat was from the sun.
7. The heat was dazzling.

8. The dazzle added to the confusion.
9. The confusion was in his mind.
10. The confusion whirled.
11. The confusion was about things.
12. The things were many.

13. His boy would be home.
14. The boy was little.
15. The boy would be watching television.
16. The television would show the race.

17. His brother would be sitting.
18. His brother would be in the stands.
19. His brother would be high up.
20. His brother would be sweating.
21. His brother would be drinking beer.
22. The beer would be warm.

23. His wife would be working.
24. She worked at the supermarket.
25. She would be checking groceries.
26. She could not hear the race.

27. The racer put on his helmet.
28. The helmet was white.
29. He fastened the strap.
30. The strap was red.
31. The strap was secure.
32. The strap was under his chin.

33. He shook his head.
34. His senses came alive.
35. The aliveness was sudden.

36. His nostrils filled.
37. They filled with an odor.
38. The odor was pungent.
39. The odor was oil.
40. The odor was carbon monoxide.

41. He looked up.
42. He saw the flag.
43. The flag was white.
44. The flag was held high.

45. He felt the steering wheel.
46. The wheel was smooth.
47. The wheel was under his hands.
48. His hands were sweaty.

49. The engine barked.
50. The barking was sharp.
51. The engine wound up.
52. The winding up was a scream.
53. The scream was high.
54. The scream was tense.

55. The flag flashed.
56. The flashing was downward.
57. His tires spun.
58. They squealed against the pavement.
59. They smoked a trail.
60. The trail was of rubber.

☞ SUGGESTION: Finish the story of the race. Or write a short paper describing your feelings just before you did something that frightened you.

Automobiles and Personality

1. The automobile is an extension.
2. The extension is of personality.
3. This extension is for many Americans.

4. It expresses an identity.
5. The expression is to others.
6. It also expresses a dream.
7. The expression is to oneself.

8. Consider the expression of identity.
9. Consider this first.

10. One example is the ordinary man.
11. The man works from 8 to 5.
12. The man lives in the suburbs.
13. The man mows his lawn.
14. The mowing is done on Saturday afternoons.

15. The man has a wife.
16. He has two or three children.
17. The children are small.

18. He buys a station wagon.
19. The wagon is big.
20. The wagon is powerful.
21. The wagon is loaded with features.
22. The features are for luxury.

23. The man is making an announcement.
24. The announcement is to the world.
25. The announcement is that he is a "family man."

26. He has settled down.
27. His life is practical.
28. His life is stable.

29. His automobile amounts to a definition.
30. The definition is of his values.
31. The values concern life.

32. The same thing holds true for the farmer.
33. The farmer buys a pickup truck.
34. The pickup is for work.
35. The work is done on the farm.

36. Often he will drive his truck to town.
37. He will leave his car at home in the garage.
38. This is because he is proud of his truck.
39. This is because he is proud of his life.

40. The truck is an expression.
41. The expression is of a way of life.
42. He values this way of life.

43. The car may be more comfortable.
44. But he does not like to drive it.
45. This is because it does not express his personality.
46. It does not express his identity.

47. Consider now the expression of dreams.
48. The expression is through automobiles.

49. Next door to the family man lives another man.
50. This man also has a wife.
51. This man also has small children.
52. This man also has a dog.
53. This man also has goldfish.
54. This man also has a barbecue.
55. This man also has a picnic table.

56. He has a house.
57. The house is like the others.
58. Its design is identical.

59. This man also works from eight to five.
60. He mows the lawn on Saturdays.
61. He lives an ordinary life.

62. But he buys a fastback.
63. He does not buy a station wagon.

64. The fastback has wheels.
65. The wheels are magnesium.
66. The wheels are for racing.
67. The fastback has a tachometer.
68. The tachometer is for racing.

69. It also has an engine.
70. The engine is for racing.
71. The engine has equipment.
72. The equipment includes fuel injection.
73. The equipment includes rocker arms.
74. The rocker arms are high-lift.
75. The equipment includes ignition.
76. The ignition is special.

77. This is all for show.
78. The man does not race.

79. His automobile is thus an expression.
80. The expresson is of a dream.
81. The dream is of a picture.
82. His picture is of another life.
83. The life would be more exciting.

84. Next door to the farmer lives another farmer.
85. This farmer does not drive his pickup to town.
86. He drives a large sedan.
87. He cannot afford it.

88. This car is large.
89. It is plush.
90. It has accessories.
91. The accessories have an association.
92. The association is with living.
93. The living is in the city.

94. The sedan is impractical.
95. It is impractical for the farm.
96. But it looks good.
97. It is good for appearances.
98. The appearances are in town.

99. It expresses his dream.
100. The dream is of a life.
101. The life would be away from the farm.

☞ SUGGESTION: Design a car for yourself that will be an expression of your personality. Or justify the purchase of a particular new car—color, body style, engine, the accessories—in terms of your personality. Or assign automobile names and characteristics to two or three people you know and explain the similarities. Or explain why, for some people, cars are no longer desirable as an extension of their personality.

Parable II

1. A seller once lived at Hangchow.
2. The seller sold fruit.
3. The seller knew how to keep oranges.
4. The oranges kept for a whole year.
5. The oranges didn't spoil.

6. The fruit always looked fresh.
7. The fruit was firm.
8. The fruit was golden.
9. But the inside was dry.
10. The dryness was like a cocoon.
11. The cocoon was old.

12. One day I told the seller my feelings.
13. His oranges were for the altar.
14. His oranges were for purposes.
15. The purposes were sacrificial.
16. His oranges were for show.

17. The seller had created an illusion.
18. The illusion was outrageous.
19. The illusion was to cheat fools.
20. The cheating was out of their money.

21. The seller replied in this way.
22. "Our officials eat the bread of state.
23. They know no shame.
24. They sit in halls.
25. The halls are lofty.
26. They ride horses.
27. The horses are fine.
28. They get drunk.
29. The drunkenness is with wine.
30. They stuff themselves.
31. The stuffing is with food.
32. The food is rich.
33. They put on looks.
34. The looks are awe-inspiring.
35. The looks are dignified."

36. "But they are a display.
37. Their display is an illusion.
38. The illusion is of greatness.
39. The illusion is of worth."

40. "The officials are dry.
41. The officials are empty.
42. The emptiness is inside."

43. Then the seller laughed at me.
44. "You pay no heed to these things.
45. These things are important."

46. "You are very particular.
47. Your concern is for things.
48. Those things are trivial."

Cesar Chavez

1. Chavez walks at the head of the crowd.
2. The crowd is restless.
3. The crowd is angry.

4. Behind him are signs.
5. The signs tell about the efforts.
6. The efforts are made by Chicanos.
7. The efforts are to get decent conditions.
8. The conditions are for working.
9. The conditions are for living.
10. The conditions are in the vineyards.

11. The scene recalls the 1930s.
12. The scene recalls the Great Depression.
13. Whites organized for survival then.
14. The organization was also in California.
15. The organization was also in agriculture.

16. But the Chicanos are protesting horrors.
17. The horrors are present day.
18. The horrors involve work.
19. The work is done by migrants.

20. Living conditions are often terrible.
21. Housing codes cause the conditions.
22. Housing codes do not apply to camps.
23. The camps are for laborers.

24. The workers live in shacks.
25. The shacks are without bathrooms.
26. The shacks are without water.

27. Often there are ten people.
28. Often there is one room.

29. The income averages under $2,000 a year.
30. The income is for a family.
31. The payment is unfair.
32. The payment is for labor.
33. The labor is backbreaking.
34. The labor is long.

35. Violations are frequent.
36. The violations are of laws.
37. The laws forbid child labor.
38. The violations are because of the wages.
39. The wages are very low.

40. The family must eat.
41. The children must work.

42. Migrant workers do not get Social Security.
43. Migrant workers do not get Workman's Compensation.
44. Migrant workers do not have health benefits.

45. Migrant workers get sick.
46. Migrant workers lose jobs.
47. Migrant workers go hungry.

48. So Chavez continues his work.
49. The work began in 1965.

50. There is much to be done.
51. The need is obvious.
52. But Chicanos are hopeful.
53. These Chicanos are many.
54. The hope is because of Chavez.

55. They see him as a man.
56. The man has vision.
57. The man has competence.
58. The competence is natural.

59. They see him as a liberator.
60. A liberator can organize Chicanos.

☞ SUGGESTION: Check in your library to find out what the results of the grape strike were. What is Chavez working on now? Write a brief report of Chavez's most recent activity.

THE GROOM

1. The groom stands in a room.
2. The room is off to the side.
3. The room is in the church.
4. He waits anxiously.
5. He tries to smile.

6. Sweat stands out on his forehead.
7. The groom wipes away the sweat.
8. The groom blinks.
9. The groom fidgets with his tie.
10. His tie is a bow.
11. His tie is black.

12. The cue comes from the organist.
13. The best man opens the door.
14. The best man follows the groom.
15. Their place is at the altar.
16. The altar is opposite the pulpit.
17. The pulpit is oak.

18. All eyes turn toward them.
19. The turning is brief.

20. The groom glances toward the rear.
21. The rear is in the church.
22. People are standing there.
23. The groom tries to smile.

24. All eyes leave the groom.
25. All eyes turn toward the doors.
26. The doors are in the rear.
27. A figure appears.
28. The figure wears silk.
29. The figure is dressed in white.
30. The figure wears lace.

31. Her bridesmaids lead the procession.
32. Her bridesmaids rustle down the aisle.
33. The bridesmaids' dresses are pastels.
34. The pastels are green.
35. The pastels are yellow.
36. The bridesmaids carry daisies.
37. The daisies are fresh.
38. The daisies smell like sunlight.

39. Music swells through the church.
40. The music is familiar.

41. There are smiles.
42. The smiles are on faces.
43. The faces approach.
44. The faces turn toward him.
45. The groom tenses his face.
46. The groom tries to look happy.
47. The groom bites his lip.

48. The father looks toward the groom.
49. The father is the bride's.
50. The father is squarish.
51. The father is shovel-faced.
52. The groom nods.

53. The bride moves next to the groom.
54. The bride's face is veiled.
55. The veil is white.
56. The veil is lace.
57. The groom clenches his fingernails.
58. The clenching is into his hands.

☞ SUGGESTION: Finish the account of this wedding. Why is the groom biting his nails and clenching his hands? As you write the rest of the story, you may want to tell the thoughts that go through the groom's mind, or you may want to shift to the bride's point of view. You might even tell the story from the point of view of someone else in the bridal party who knows the background of what is happening.

Up, Up, and Away

1. The junior executives are young.
2. They are freshly combed.
3. They work their way.
4. The way is into the elevator.

5. The door closes behind the last man.
6. The close is with a hiss.
7. The hiss is soft.
8. The hiss is faintly mocking.

9. The elevator begins to lift.
10. The lift is with a hum.
11. The hum is electric.

12. Their eyes are fixed on the numbers.
13. The numbers are above the door.
14. The numbers move from left to right.
15. The numbers click off in sequence.

16. The junior executives have differences.
17. But the differences are minor.
18. Their similarities are striking.

19. Each has a face.
20. The face is earnest.
21. The face shows ambition.
22. The ambition is youthful.

23. Each has a similar style collar.
24. The collar is worn with a tie.
25. The tie is striped.
26. The tie is softly muted.
27. The tie is asserted by a stickpin.
28. The stickpin is bold.

29. Each has a sportcoat.
30. The sportcoat is plaid.
31. It is matched to slacks.
32. The slacks are trim.
33. The slacks are cuffless.

34. Each has an attache case.
35. The case is part of the uniform.

36. And each has a look.
37. The look is as if he is stamped out.
38. A mold does the stamping.
39. A mold makes everyone well rounded.
40. A mold makes everyone fit.
41. The fitting is into the machinery.
42. The fitting is smooth.

43. Their lives are greased.
44. Their lives are grooved.

45. But they are on their way.
46. The way is shoulder to shoulder.
47. The way is back to belly.

48. Their way is up.
49. And they travel in an elevator.
50. The elevator is also greased and grooved.

51. The elevator is symbolic.
52. The elevator mirrors the Big Elevator.
53. The Big Elevator is called The Establishment.

☞ SUGGESTION: Consider the question of whether your life is "greased and grooved." Where do you hope to be a year from now? five years? ten? twenty? Why?

Stereotypes

1. Stereotyping is a way of thinking.
2. The thinking is about groups.
3. The groups are people.
4. Everybody is in the group.
5. Everybody is alike.

6. Stereotyping emphasizes similarities.
7. The similarities are in the group.
8. Stereotyping ignores differences.
9. The differences are in the group.

10. One belief is about redhaired people.
11. Redhaired people are hot-tempered.
12. The belief is a stereotype.

13. Another belief is about Scotsmen.
14. Scotsmen are stingy.
15. The belief is a stereotype.

16. Stereotyping lumps people together.
17. People are alike.
18. The likeness is in one thing.
19. Being alike makes them alike.
20. The likeness is in all things.

21. Such thinking ignores many redheads.
22. Many redheads are even-tempered.

23. Such thinking ignores many Scotsmen.
24. Many Scotsmen are generous.

25. Stereotyping emphasizes differences.
26. The differences are between groups.
27. Stereotyping ignores similarities.
28. The similarities are to other people.

29. Stereotyping forgets.
30. Many blondes lose their tempers.
31. Many brunettes lose their tempers too.

32. Stereotyping forgets.
33. Many Americans are stingy.
34. Many Brazilians are stingy.
35. Many Frenchmen are stingy too.

36. Stereotyping redheads does little harm.
37. Stereotyping Scotsmen does little harm.
38. Stereotyping redheads leads to jokes.
39. Stereotyping redheads leads to kidding.
40. Stereotyping Scotsmen leads to jokes.
41. Stereotyping Scotsmen leads to kidding.

42. But stereotyping is usually inaccurate.
43. Stereotyping is always simple-minded.
44. Stereotyping is sometimes dangerous.

45. The danger lies in separation.
46. The separation is between people.
47. The separation comes from exaggeration.
48. The exaggeration is of differences.
49. The differences are in color.
50. The differences are in nationality.
51. The differences are in religion.
52. The differences are in language.

53. The separation forgets our similarities.
54. The similarities are fundamental.
55. The similarities are human.

56. We exaggerate differences.
57. We ignore things.
58. The things are what we share.
59. We become prejudiced.

60. Prejudice grows out of fear.
61. Prejudice grows out of hatred.
62. Prejudice leads to fear.
63. Prejudice leads to hatred.

64. Racism is one kind of prejudice.
65. Racism is harmful.
66. The harmfulness is extreme.

67. Racists can be any color.
68. Racists can be white.
69. Racists can be black.
70. Racists can be brown.
71. Racists can be red.
72. Racists can be yellow.

73. A white man is a racist.
74. The white man thinks about blacks.
75. Blacks are all alike.

76. So is a black a racist.
77. The black thinks about Chinese.
78. Chinese are all alike.

79. So is a Chinese a racist.
80. The Chinese thinks about white men.
81. The white men are all alike.

82. The likeness is in something.
83. The racist hates something.
84. The racist feels contempt for something.

85. Then the racist has something.
86. The something is tangible.
87. The something can be pointed at.
88. The something can be discriminated against.
89. The something can be spat on.
90. The something can be attacked.

91. The attack comes from fear.
92. The fear is of differences.
93. The differences are not really important.

94. The hatred is expressed in labels.
95. There are examples.
96. The examples are of labels.
97. Labels are "chink."
98. Labels are "nigger."
99. Labels are "honky."
100. Labels are "wop."
101. Labels are "kike."
102. Labels are "gook."

103. Labeling tells us something.
104. The something is about people.
105. People use labels.
106. People think in stereotypes.
107. The stereotyping is simple-minded.

☞ SUGGESTION: Examine one of your own prejudices to see whether it grew out of a ready-made stereotype or whether something that happened to you led to your creation of a stereotype. If the prejudice comes from a personal experience, examine the incident to see what happened to your thinking. Or has anyone else ever stereotyped you? How did the stereotyping make you feel?

Water Skier

1. The water skier sits on the float.
2. He waits.
3. His muscles are tensed.

4. The boat lurches forward.
5. The rope tightens the slack.
6. The rope drags the skier.
7. The drag is through the water.

8. Suddenly he is up.
9. He leans to one side.
10. He veers outward.

11. He dips.
12. He glides.
13. A spray trails behind him.
14. The spray is silver in the sunshine.

15. His hair flattens.
16. The flattening is against his forehead.
17. He sees his reflection.
18. The reflection is on the water.

19. The surface is glass.
20. The glass is liquid.
21. The glass gleams.
22. The glass glitters.

23. He stiffens.
24. He locks one leg.
25. He lifts a ski.
26. He leans back.

27. His ski tip hits a wave.
28. It shatters the calm.
29. It breaks his reflection.
30. The breaking is a spray of foam.
31. The pieces fade behind him.

32. Now the skier signals "in."
33. The boat makes a turn.
34. The turn is wide.

35. The boat heads toward shore.
36. The heading is direct.
37. The boat is moving.
38. The moving is rapid.

39. The boat swerves.
40. The swerve is sudden.
41. The swerve is away from the beach.

42. The skier glides to the beach.
43. He sinks slowly.
44. The sinking is into water.
45. The water is green.

46. He feels the wash.
47. The wash is from the boat.
48. The wash laps at his back.

☞ NOTE: In "Water Skier," longer sentences will add to the feeling of movement. Try combining sentences 8–10 and 11–14. And if you're really experimental, try putting sentences 32–34, 35–38, and 39–41 into a single sentence.

Dilemma

1. A dilemma is a problem.
2. The problem has two solutions.
3. Both solutions are bad.

4. The Nuremberg War Trials followed World War II.
5. The trials posed a dilemma.
6. The dilemma was for individuals.
7. The individuals were thoughtful.
8. The individuals were all over the world.

9. The trials judged Nazi officers.
10. The officers were involved.
11. The involvement was in the execution.
12. The execution was of six million Jews.
13. The Jews were in concentration camps.
14. The concentration camps were German.

15. The prosecution argued.
16. The officers were guilty.
17. The guilt was for crimes.
18. The crimes were against humanity.
19. The officers had a responsibility.
20. The responsibility was to the human race.

21. The defense argued.
22. The officers were not responsible.
23. The officers were carrying out orders.
24. The orders were from the "high command."
25. The high command was Hitler specifically.

26. Many officers were found guilty.
27. Their guilt was war crimes.
28. The officers were sentenced to death.
29. The officers were sentenced to imprisonment.

30. The problem is clear.
31. The solution is not.

32. Any human being deplores war.
33. Any human being deplores suffering.
34. The suffering is human.
35. Any human being deplores destruction.
36. The destruction is senseless.

37. And any human being fears punishment.
38. A human being is punished for disobeying.
39. He disobeys orders.
40. People give orders.
41. The people are in power.

42. The problem is clear.
43. The solution is not.

44. Should an individual disobey orders?
45. The individual risks punishment.
46. Should an individual follow orders?
47. The orders conflict.
48. The conflict is with his conscience.

☞ SUGGESTION: Can you see any similarity between the Nuremberg War Trials and some of the problems that have come out of the Vietnam war? If you were faced with a dilemma like this, what do you think you would do? Be sure to explain the reasons behind your decision.

BIG ADA

1. Every town has drifters.
2. The drifters come.
3. The drifters go.
4. The drifters do not leave a mark.
5. Ada left hers.

6. Ada was a town character.
7. Ada was enormous.
8. The enormousness was across the buttocks.
9. Everyone called her "Big Ada."

10. No one knew her real name.
11. No one knew her age.

12. She lived in an apartment.
13. The apartment was over a tavern.
14. The tavern was on Main Street.
15. She worked in the tavern.
16. She sang folk songs.
17. She played a guitar.
18. The guitar was hers.

19. She wore a jacket.
20. The jacket was fringed.
21. She wore a hat.
22. The hat was for cowboys.
23. The hat had a crown.
24. The crown was high.
25. She wore pants.
26. The pants were Western.
27. She wore boots.
28. The boots had pointed toes.

29. She roamed the town.
30. The roaming was in the afternoon.
31. She sat in front of a drugstore.
32. She talked to children.
33. She listened.
34. The listening was to their adventures.

35. She sang.
36. The singing was to the children.
37. She told stories.
38. The stories were for the children.
39. She helped them.
40. The helping was when they were troubled.

41. Ada was warm.
42. Ada was friendly.
43. Ada was a teacher.
44. Her teaching was the best.
45. Her teaching was natural.

46. Ada left.
47. No one knew why.

48. There was only one clue.
49. The clue was to her disappearance.
50. The sheriff found the clue.
51. It was in a basket.
52. The basket was for trash.
53. The basket was in Ada's room.

54. The clue was crumpled.
55. The clue was a scrap.
56. The scrap was of a napkin.
57. The napkin had been drawn on.

58. The drawing showed a figure.
59. The figure seemed to be trapped.
60. The trap was a box.
61. Or the trap was a cage.
62. The trap had bars.

63. People wondered about the drawing.
64. What did the box symbolize?
65. What did the bars symbolize?

66. The questions still linger.
67. The questions are still unanswered.

☞ SUGGESTION: What do you think the drawing meant? Write a paragraph or two giving your explanation of the drawing and the reasons Ada left town. (You may be interested to know that Big Ada was—and perhaps still is—a real person.)

Picnic

1. We made our way.
2. The way was along the edge.
3. The edge was of the river.
4. The edge was rocky.
5. The edge was green.
6. The greenness was weeds.
7. The weeds were low growing.

8. We ducked.
9. The ducking was under branches.
10. The branches were shadowy.
11. We tried to keep our balance.

12. It had been an afternoon.
13. The afternoon was delicious.

14. The sun had come off the water.
15. The sun had glinted.
16. The sun had glittered.
17. The glittering was in the eddies.
18. The eddies were green.
19. The green was reflection.

20. There had just been the sounds.
21. The sounds were lazy.
22. The sounds were insects.
23. The sounds were leaves.
24. The sounds were us.

25. The whole afternoon had unfolded.
26. The unfolding was natural.
27. The unfolding was into sunlight.
28. The unfolding was into shadows.

29. We had tossed rocks.
30. The rocks went into the river.
31. The rocks hit the water.
32. The hitting made a splash.
33. The splash was white.

34. Then we had watched a man.
35. The man was downstream.
36. The man waded out.
37. The man went into the water.
38. The man worked his way.
39. The way was over the rocks.
40. The rocks were slimy.
41. The sliminess was algae.

42. His lure had made an arc.
43. The arc was short.
44. His lure trailed a filament.
45. The filament was invisible.
46. His lure dropped into the water.
47. The drop made no ripple.

48. The current had taken the lure.
49. The lure went under the trees.
50. The lure went toward a pool.
51. The pool was quiet.
52. The pool was green.

53. The man had tried repeatedly.
54. He had whipped his line.
55. The line went into the current.
56. But he had not gotten a bite.

57. Finally he had left.
58. We were left to each other.
59. We were left to our sandwiches.
60. The sandwiches were of peanut butter.

61. We had talked.
62. We had listened to the rhythms.
63. The rhythms were in the afternoon.
64. The rhythms seemed part of us.

65. Then we had unpacked our poles.
66. The poles were for fishing.
67. The unpacking was just before leaving.

68. There was one cast each.
69. The lines whirred out.
70. The lines went through the reels.

71. And then light had come bouncing.
72. The light bounced off the water.
73. The water was alive.
74. The water thrashed.
75. The thrashing was white.

76. It was the end.
77. The end was to the day.
78. The end was fitting.
79. The day was memorable.

80. Two trout were blanketed.
81. The trout were called rainbow.
82. The blanketing was with ferns.
83. The ferns were green.
84. The ferns were sweet smelling.

85. We had smiled at each other.
86. We had started making our way.
87. The way was down the river.
88. The way was toward the trail.
89. The trail would take us back.
90. Back was to the car.

91. And so now we were climbing.
92. The climb angled up from the riverbank.
93. The climb angled into the hush.
94. The hush was pine smell.
95. The pine smell washed down from the hill.
96. The pine smell mixed with the harshness.
97. The harshness was juniper.
98. The harshness was sage.

99. Everything seemed good.
100. Everything seemed worth remembering.

101. There was pine.
102. There was shadow.
103. There was the crack.
104. The crack was twigs.
105. The twigs were underfoot.

106. We did not think of the smell.
107. The smell was smoke.
108. The smoke was from diesels.
109. The smell was dust.
110. The dust was in the city.

☞ NOTE: In "Picnic," notice that you are working with two different time periods. One is the time of leaving, in sentences 1–11 and sentences 91–110. The other is the picnic itself, which is remembered in sentences 12–90, the big middle section. This technique is called "flashback."

☞ SUGGESTION: Try using flashback in describing some experience of your own. You might write about your return to some place you have not seen for a long time, or you might just remember some incident that occurred earlier. You will not have a flashback, however, unless you begin and end with a time or place different from the one in the middle.

Chicano Movement

1. The Chicano movement results from attempts.
2. Mexican-Americans make the attempts.
3. The attempts are to find identity.
4. The identity is cultural.

5. Their aims are social.
6. Their aims are political.
7. Their aims are similar.
8. The similarities are of hopes.
9. The hopes are shared by all minorities.

10. Chicanos want to assert themselves.
11. Chicanos want to establish control.
12. They want to control institutions.
13. The institutions affect their lives.

14. Chicanos want to preserve their heritage.
15. Their heritage is a mixture.
16. The mixture is cultural.
17. The mixture is Spanish.
18. The mixture is Indian.

19. Chicanos want to promote self-awareness.
20. Chicanos want to promote pride.
21. Chicanos want to promote cooperation.
22. The cooperation is in their communities.
23. The pride is in their communities.

24. Chicanos want to encourage a use.
25. The use is widespread.
26. The use is of "Pocho."
27. "Pocho" is a mixture.
28. The mixture is of language.
29. The language is Spanish.
30. The language is English.

31. Chicanos want to stimulate expression.
32. The expression is literary.
33. The expression is in newspapers.
34. The newspapers are Chicano.
35. The expression is in magazines.
36. The magazines are Chicano.

37. Chicanos want to encourage studies.
38. The studies are Chicano.
39. The studies provide understanding.
40. The understanding is of their past.

41. Chicanos want to have a voice.
42. The voice is in textbooks.
43. Their children read the textbooks.

44. Chicanos want to exert pressure.
45. The pressure is through publicity.
46. The publicity is to force an awakening.
47. The awakening is of Anglos.

48. Chicanos want opportunities.
49. The opportunities are for education.
50. The opportunities are for employment.
51. The opportunities are for self-respect.

☞ NOTE: Sometimes paragraphs can be effectively organized by repeating a sentence pattern. This repetition is especially useful for listing a series of ideas. Such repetition is also used by political speech-writers because it sets up a rhythm or "chant." Such repetition can be overused, of course, or used just to create emotion, but the old rule about "like things said in like ways" is probably worth remembering.

☞ SUGGESTION: If you are interested in what the Chicano movement is doing, you might use this essay as an introduction for a paper in which you discuss in detail one specific goal Chicanos are working toward—the use of Pocho, the language problem in elementary schools, the development of Chicano newspapers or magazines, for instance. You should be able to find information on any of these things by looking in the *Reader's Guide to Periodical Literature*.

THE CARVER

1. The carver carves wood.
2. The carver sits in the shadows.
3. His shoulders are hunched.
4. His face is calm.
5. His mouth is a line.
6. The line is thin-lipped.
7. The line shows concentration.

8. Chips surround him.
9. The chips are wood.
10. The chips are curls.
11. The curls are white.
12. The curls smell sweet.
13. The curls litter the earth.
14. The earth is brown.
15. The earth is hard packed.

16. The carver watches the wood.
17. An eyebrow emerges.

18. His knife peels away the skin.
19. The skin is wood.
20. A bone begins to protrude.
21. The bone is along the cheek.

22. Lips unfold.
23. The lips are thin.
24. The lips are concentrated.
25. The unfolding is slow.
26. Chips fall to the side.

27. Smells drift in.
28. The smells are of orchards.
29. The orchards are blossoming.
30. The blossoms are white.
31. The smells bring memories.
32. The memories are of faces.
33. The faces are in another time.
34. The time is long past.

35. The shavings fall.
36. The falling is from the face.
37. The face is the carving.
38. Its texture is rough.
39. Its lines are bold.
40. Its lines are clean.

41. Its eyes stare into space.
42. The eyes are wide.
43. The eyes are deep set.

44. The nose is straight.
45. The nose is flared.
46. The flaring is at the bottom.
47. The flaring is above the mouth.
48. The mouth is grim.
49. The mouth is patient.

50. Then the carver lifts his carving.
51. He brushes away the shavings.
52. He examines the carving.
53. The examination is with care.
54. The care is that of a craftsman.

55. His lips relax.
56. The relaxing is a half-smile
57. The carved lips remain grim.
58. The carved lips remain patient.

59. The carver has recreated a piece.
60. The piece is of the past.

☞ SUGGESTION: Write a detailed description of someone you have seen deeply absorbed in something he likes doing. You might write about someone playing a musical instrument, someone tending a garden, someone working on his bicycle, but whatever you choose, make sure you let your reader "see" both the worker and the work he is involved in.

Returnable Bottle

1. A trend seems to be increasing.
2. The increase is across the country.
3. The trend is to use bottles.
4. The bottles are returnable.
5. The bottles are for soft drinks.
6. The bottles are for beer.

7. Environmentalists support this trend.
8. Their support is strong.

9. Environmentalists see it as a method.
10. The method is positive.
11. The method is effective.
12. The method is to reduce litter.
13. The litter is from throwaways.
14. The throwaways are bottles.
15. The throwaways are cans.

16. But the industry objects to this trend.
17. The industry makes containers.

18. The trend could cause reductions.
19. The reductions would be in jobs.
20. The jobs could number 100,000.
21. Throwaways represent half the production.
22. The production is of all bottles.
23. The production is of all cans.

24. And brewers object to returnables.
25. Their machinery is set up.
26. The set up is for throwaways.
27. The machinery represents millions.
28. The millions are of dollars.

29. Even some grocers object to returnables.
30. Their objection is because of inconvenience.
31. They face the inconvenience.
32. The inconvenience is handling returnables.
33. The inconvenience is sorting returnables.

34. Environmentalists argue.
35. The argument is in four ways.

36. A deposit would reduce littering.
37. A deposit would encourage the reuse.
38. The reusing would be of containers.

39. Returnables would reduce collection.
40. The collection is of trash.
41. The reduction would be 10 percent.
42. The 10 percent would be in many cities.
43. The 10 percent would be a savings.
44. The savings would be $200 million.

45. Returnables would conserve materials.
46. The materials are raw.
47. Returnables would conserve energy.
48. The energy is for making bottles.
49. The energy is for making cans.

50. Returnables would save the consumer.
51. The savings would be from 5 to 15 percent.
52. The 5 to 15 percent is for beer.
53. The savings would from 15 to 30 percent.
54. The 15 to 30 percent is for soft drinks.

☞ SUGGESTION: Write a conclusion for this essay that makes clear to the reader what the issues are. Then finish by saying what you think should be done about the problem. As you write your conclusion, try to avoid using phrases such as, "Now, personally, I think that . . ." or "As you can see. . . ." Such phrases would not fit with the tone of the rest of the essay.

Runaway

1. The runaway walks the streets.
2. The streets are in the city.
3. They are unfamiliar.
4. They are almost hostile.
5. He watches the neon lights.
6. They flicker against the sky.
7. They crackle against the sky.
8. The sky is grayish brown.
9. The grayish brown is the color of concrete.

10. The traffic flows by.
11. It makes him blink.

12. His tiredness is an ache.
13. The ache stretches down his back.
14. It reaches into his ankle bones.
15. It numbs his feet.

16. He leans against a building.
17. The ache is still there.

18. Buildings rise up.
19. The rising is tall.
20. The rising is angular.
21. The rising is against the evening sky.
22. The sky is getting darker.

23. He stares at the windows.
24. They are dark.
25. They are faceless in the light.
26. The light is dying.

27. It is his first night.
28. He is on the road.
29. He is in the city.
30. He is lonely.
31. He is half-afraid.

32. It was not like his dream.
33. The dream was of how it would be.

34. He had dreamed of excitement.
35. He had dreamed of money.
36. He had dreamed of freedom.

37. He had seen himself.
38. He was in the middle of the city.
39. He was moving through crowds.
40. He was like a movie hero.

41. But it was not like that.

42. He did not know where to go.
43. He did not know how to get there.
44. He was afraid to ask.
45. He did not know what to ask.

46. His walking had covered four blocks.
47. The blocks were around his hotel.
48. The blocks all looked the same.

49. He had sipped a cup.
50. The cup was of coffee.
51. The sipping was for something to do.

52. The bums had looked him over.
53. The bums were in the restaurant.
54. The restaurant was dingy.
55. One bum had coaxed a quarter.
56. The coaxing was from him.

57. Now he glanced.
58. The glancing was at a streetsign.
59. He turned.
60. He started moving down the sidewalk.
61. He moved toward his hotel.

62. He thought about his room.
63. It was narrow.
64. It was high-ceilinged.
65. It smelled like cigars.
66. The smell was stale.

67. Tomorrow was another day.
68. He would find something to do.
69. He did not know what it would be.

70. He could maybe go to a movie.
71. He could maybe make some friends.

72. There must be a lot to do.
73. He thought.
74. He pushed his hands.
75. The pushing was deep.
76. The deepness was in his pockets.
77. He tried to smile.

☞ SUGGESTION: Make a two-column list of the things that people "run away from" and "run toward." Then write a paper explaining what you discovered or what you thought about as you made the list.

Air Pollution

1. Air pollution is a problem.
2. The problem is serious.
3. The problem is man made.
4. The problem has reached a point.
5. The point is a crisis.
6. The crisis affects destiny.
7. The destiny is ours.
8. The destiny is our children's.

9. Something must be done.
10. The doing must be now.
11. The doing must be before it is too late.

12. Inaction will result in disaster.
13. Specialists predict the disaster.
14. The specialists study the atmosphere.
15. The specialists study the environment.

16. These specialists predict death.
17. Death will come within twenty years.
18. The death will be in the cities.
19. The death will be from asphyxiation.

20. Numbers will die.
21. The numbers will be great.
22. Death will occur under conditions.
23. The conditions will be in the atmosphere.
24. The conditions are called "inversions."

25. The people will suffocate.
26. Garbage will cause the suffocation.
27. The garbage is in the air.
28. The garbage is man produced.

29. Efforts must begin now.
30. The efforts must be to clear the air.
31. Pollutants must be cleared.
32. The pollutants are harmful.
33. The harm is to our health.
34. The harm is to our well-being.
35. The well-being is physical.

36. Legislators must pass laws.
37. The laws must be strict.
38. The laws must carry penalties.
39. The penalties are for polluters.
40. The penalties must be strong.

41. Industry must comply.
42. The compliance must be with measures.
43. The measures must be preventive.
44. The measures must decrease the discharge.
45. The discharge is of emissions.
46. The discharge is into the atmosphere.

47. Manufacturers must comply.
48. The manufacturers make automobiles.
49. The compliance must be with research.
50. The research must be stepped up.
51. The research must be on devices.
52. The devices clean up combustion.
53. The combustion is internal.
54. The combustion is in engines.

55. Efforts must be made.
56. Efforts must be increased.
57. The efforts are to gain cooperation.
58. The cooperation must be from citizens.
59. The citizens are average.
60. Citizens often make matters worse.
61. Citizens waste electric power.
62. Citizens burn trash.
63. Citizens do not use public transportation.
64. Citizens buy automobiles.
65. The automobiles are over-sized.

66. Everyone must be made aware.
67. The awareness must be of pollution.
68. The pollution is in the atmosphere.

69. Pollution has causes.
70. The causes are man-made.
71. The causes can be dealt with.
72. People work together.
73. The working is to solve the problem.

74. Cooperation must begin.
75. The beginning must be now.
76. Tomorrow will be too late.

☞ SUGGESTION: This essay stays fairly general. Before anything can really be done, we must stop wringing our hands and get down to cases. Draft a statement that identifies a specific idea or two for helping to create a cleaner environment. On automobile pollution, for instance, should there be a law against owning more than one car? Should all cars have smaller engines? Should bicycle paths be constructed in cities? Should cities be closed to private cars? Should gas be rationed? Should people who use public transportation get tax exemptions? What other specific proposals can you think of? Be definite about how your proposals would work. (You don't, of course, have to deal with automobile pollution.)

White Christmas

1. The light glared.
2. The light was from a globe.
3. The globe had no covering.
4. The glaring was white.
5. The glaring was in the middle.
6. The middle was in the room.

7. The room was almost empty.
8. The room had a mattress.
9. The mattress had no bedstead.
10. The mattress had no blankets.
11. The room had a basin.
12. The basin was for washing.
13. The basin was white.

14. There was a pan.
15. The pan was for frying.
16. The pan was blackened.
17. Utensils were in the pan.
18. The utensils were broken.
19. The utensils were stained.
20. The utensils were unwashed.

21. Smoke swirled.
22. The swirling was dark.
23. The swirling was in the fireplace.
24. Flames licked at the wood.
25. The wood was charred.
26. The wood was pieces.
27. The pieces were from a bedstead.

28. But the fire gave no heat.

29. People huddled.
30. The people were two.
31. The people were close.
32. The closeness was to the fire.

33. The woman had hair.
34. The hair was blonde.
35. The hair was turning.
36. The turning was to gray.
37. The hair was pulled back.
38. The pulling was tight.
39. The pulling was into a bun.
40. Her face was pale.
41. Her face was lined.
42. The lines were deep.

43. The man had a face.
44. The face was red.
45. The face was chapped.
46. The face scowled.

47. Their breath was white.
48. Their breath was frosted.
49. They were silent.
50. They were waiting.
51. The wait was for food.
52. The food was due to arrive.
53. The arrival would be soon.
54. The arrival would be from the Salvation Army.

55. The man reached over to touch.
56. The reaching was to his wife.
57. She sat.
58. She did not move.
59. Her hands were folded.
60. The folding was in her lap.

61. Then she looked up.
62. The looking was with a smile.
63. The smile was tired.

64. "I'm dreaming of a white Christmas."
65. The woman murmured.

☞ SUGGESTION: In this sketch, there is an ironic contrast between the Christmas described and the kind of celebration we usually associate with "White Christmas." Write a "White Christmas" from your own memory—either cheerful or sad.

New Schools

1. Educators are experimenting.
2. The experimenting is across the country.
3. The experimenting is today.
4. The experimenting is with a concept.
5. The concept is new.
6. The concept is called "open education."

7. Open education offers a way.
8. The way is different.
9. The way is to help people.
10. The help is to develop ability.
11. The ability is natural.
12. The ability is theirs.
13. The way is enjoyable.

14. Open schools are committed.
15. These schools are new.
16. The commitment is to learning.
17. The learning is continuous.
18. The learning is individual.

19. They do not want "assemblylines."
20. "Assemblylines" make learning a function.
21. The function is of time.
22. The time is put in.
23. The "assemblylines" last for twelve years.

24. New schools reject this concept.
25. The concept is traditional.
26. The concept is educational.

27. They have beliefs.
28. The beliefs seem radical.

29. New schools have a belief.
30. The belief is about learning.
31. Learning should be fun.
32. Learning should not be a kind of work.
33. That kind of work is hard.
34. That kind of work is dull.

35. New schools have a belief.
36. The belief is about school.
37. School should be part of the community.
38. School should not be separate from the community.

39. School should respond.
40. The response should be to needs.
41. The needs are the community's.
42. The response should be to problems.
43. The problems are the community's.
44. The needs should be expressed.
45. The problems should be expressed.

46. New schools have a belief.
47. The belief is about levels.
48. The levels are grades.
49. The levels are bad.
50. The levels separate people.
51. The separation is by age.
52. The separation is by ability.

53. School should not define categories.
54. The categories are grade levels.
55. The categories are subject matter.
56. Categories interfere with learning.
57. Categories shut doors.

58. New schools have a belief.
59. The belief is about schools.
60. Schools should open doors.
61. Schools should not close doors.

62. Schools should encourage creativity.
63. Schools should encourage problem solving.
64. Schools should encourage decision making.
65. Schools should encourage independence.
66. The independence is in thinking.

67. Schools should help people.
68. The help is learning.
69. The learning is cooperation.

70. New schools have a belief.
71. Everyone is a student.
72. Everyone is a teacher.

73. Six-year-olds help teach.
74. Six-year-olds teach three-year-olds.
75. Three-year-olds learn things.
76. The things are getting along.
77. The getting along is with others.
78. The things are sharing.
79. The sharing is with others.

80. Fifty-year-olds learn things.
81. Fifty-year-olds learn from teenagers.
82. Fifty-year-olds learn how to do things.
83. The things are playing guitars.
84. The things are making pottery.

85. Doctors learn from mechanics.
86. The mechanics have skills.
87. The skills are sophisticated.
88. The skills are for "doctoring."
89. Engines are "doctored."

90. Children learn reading.
91. The reading is taught by tutors.
92. The reading is taught by machines.
93. The reading is taught by their friends.
94. The reading is taught by housewives.
95. The reading is taught by experts.
96. The experts are well trained.

97. Specialists help individuals.
98. The individuals may have problems.
99. The problems are learning.
100. Specialists keep track of progress.

101. Children learn botany.
102. Children grow tomatoes.
103. Children grow marigolds.

104. Children learn ecology.
105. Children collect newspapers.
106. The newspapers are old.
107. Children sell newspapers.
108. The selling is to plants.
109. The plants recycle paper.

110. Learning becomes a free-for-all.
111. The free-for-all is wild.
112. The free-for-all is happy.

113. Learning becomes a process.
114. The process is life long.
115. The process is growing.
116. The process is becoming.
117. The learning is in new schools.

☞ SUGGESTION: Write a paper comparing the way you learned geography—or arithmetic, art, or whatever you like—with the way you think it might be learned in a new school.

Incident

1. The man slumps against the bar.
2. He sips his drink.
3. It is the height of the evening.

4. He is a worker.
5. He works in construction.
6. He wears his hat.
7. The hat is hard.
8. The hat is worn everywhere.

9. The hat is like a badge.
10. The badge identifies him.
11. The identification is to the world.
12. The identification is to himself.

13. His face is young looking.
14. It is weathered.
15. The weathering is by the sun.
16. His face has started to show its age.
17. Age shows at the corners of his eyes.
18. Age shows around his mouth.

19. His eyes are unfocused.
20. His eyes are glassy.

21. Sounds surround him.
22. The surrounding is like a web.
23. The sounds are voices.
24. The sounds are vibrations.
25. The vibrations mumble from the jukebox.

26. His brain feels dizzy.
27. It feels veiled from the world.
28. It feels as if it were wrapped.
29. The wrapping is in gauze.
30. The gauze is white.

31. He tips his drink.
32. A grin spreads.
33. It cracks his face.
34. Then it fades.

35. He is confused.
36. His eyes close.
37. His eyes are puffy.
38. His eyes surrender.
39. The surrender is to dizziness.

40. He mumbles.
41. The mumbling is to himself.
42. "A little sleep.
43. A little shuteye."

44. He knows one thing.
45. Fatigue leaves when sleep comes.
46. So does dizziness.

47. He stands up.
48. He leans against the bar.
49. The bar is covered with glasses.
50. The glasses are stained.
51. The glasses are empty.

52. The bartender stands behind the bar.
53. He wipes glasses.
54. The wiping is with a dishtowel.
55. The towel is torn.

56. The worker sips at his drink.
57. The drink is warm.
58. The drink is flat.
59. The worker eyes the bartender.

60. The worker demands another drink.
61. The bartender winks.
62. The bartender speaks.
63. "No more."
64. The bartender keeps wiping the glass.
65. It is the same glass.

66. The man yells.
67. "Another drink!"
68. The bartender turns away.
69. The bartender seems deaf.

70. The man stares at a back.
71. The back belongs to the bartender.
72. The man feels something bristle.
73. The bristling is hot.
74. The hotness is inside him.
75. The hotness churns.

76. The bartender looks like a bear.
77. His shirt is pulled out.
78. His shirt hangs loose.
79. His shirt hangs over his hips.
80. The hips are soft.
81. The hips are lazy.

82. The worker starts around a corner.
83. The corner is the bar.
84. The bartender turns.
85. The bartender has something.
86. The something is in his hand.
87. The something is small.
88. The something is dark.
89. The something is menacing.
90. The something is pointed at the worker.

91. The worker stops.
92. His mouth is open.
93. The worker blinks at the gun.
94. The gun is snub-nosed.
95. The gun is deadly looking.

96. He shrugs his shoulders.
97. He manages a smile.
98. The smile is weak.
99. He says something.
100. "What the hell?"

101. Then he heads for the door.
102. He walks sideways.
103. He bumps into tables.

☞ SUGGESTION: Describe some scene you have seen in a restaurant or on the street. Try to use as many definite details as have been used in this essay.

Alcohol and Marijuana

1. There is much talk.
2. The talking occurs today.
3. The talking is about evils.
4. The evils are from marijuana.

5. But few people talk about alcohol.
6. Alcohol represents a hazard.
7. The hazard is to health.
8. The hazard is greater than marijuana.

9. Consider an example.
10. Consider our consumption.
11. The consumption is of alcohol.

12. The nations drinks 650 million gallons.
13. The gallons are distilled spirits.
14. The drinking is done each year.

15. Americans guzzle 100 million barrels.
16. The barrels contain beer.
17. The guzzling is done each year.

18. We also drink wine.
19. The volume is 200 million gallons.

20. Such drinking produces hangovers.
21. The hangovers are many.
22. But it also produces some statistics.
23. The statistics are sobering.

24. Six million Americans are alcoholics.
25. Or six million Americans are chronic users.

26. Drunkenness leads to 30 to 50 percent of all arrests made.
27. The arrests are on the average.
28. The average is national.

29. Cirrhosis ranks sixth.
30. The ranking is causes of death.
31. Cirrhosis is a disease.
32. The disease affects the liver.
33. Alcohol causes cirrhosis.

34. Damage results in psychosis.
35. Damage is to the brain.
36. The damage is irreversible.
37. Drinking causes the damage.

38. Alcohol is a factor.
39. The factor is in accidents.
40. Automobiles have accidents.
41. The factor is from 50 to 70 percent.

42. These are the facts.
43. The facts are cold.

44. But people lecture pot smokers.
45. The lecture is about the evils.
46. The evils are from marijuana.

47. Marijuana should be legalized.
48. The legalization should be complete.
49. The legalization should be immediate.

☞ SUGGESTION: Has the writer shown that alcohol is more dangerous than marijuana? He concludes that marijuana should be legalized, but has he shown why? This paper might be an argument for making alcohol illegal, but what does it prove about marijuana? If you think marijuana should be legalized, write a paper giving some different reasons for your belief. If you think it should remain illegal, write a paper giving reasons for that belief.

Shoeshine Boy

1. The Boy is a man.
2. The Boy works at the airport.
3. He shines shoes for the travelers.
4. The travelers come and go.
5. They are always impatient.
6. They are always in a big hurry.

7. The Boy is white.
8. He might be black.
9. He might be Indian.
10. He might be Puerto Rican.
11. He might be Mexican.

12. The place might be any place.
13. The time might be any time.
14. The Boy might be any man.
15. His job is shoes.
16. He works at it six days a week.

17. He has been at it for years.
18. He has watched the travelers.
19. The travelers come by the thousands.
20. The travelers have faces.
21. Their faces are nameless.

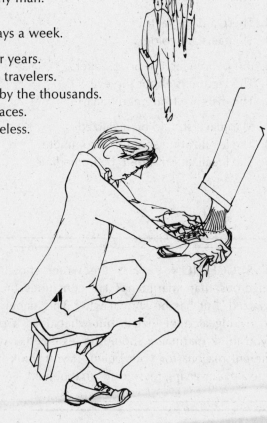

22. He works fast.
23. He works methodically.
24. He knows that time is money.

25. His head bends over his work.
26. His tongue darts between his teeth.

27. His hands are quick.
28. His hands are trained.
29. Their training is in the routine.
30. The routine is working up a shine.

31. And the routine does not vary.

32. A traveler sits down in the chair.
33. The chair is elevated.
34. The chair is high-backed.
35. The chair is like a throne.

36. The Boy eyes the shoes.
37. He inspects the leather.
38. The inspection is with scorn.
39. The scorn is faint.
40. The scorn is almost a sneer.
41. He reaches for his brush.
42. The brush is for cleaning.

43. The brush makes circles.
44. The circles are across the leather.
45. The circles are soapy.

46. The Boy wipes the shoes.
47. Wiping makes them dull but clean.

48. He reaches for his wax.
49. He skims off a film.
50. The skimming is with his fingertips.
51. The film is applied to the shoes.
52. The application is with strokes.
53. The strokes are quick.
54. The strokes are back and forth.

55. He brushes at the leather.
56. The brushing is with his palms.
57. He works the leather.
58. The working makes a shine.
59. The shine is dull.

60. He then squeezes a rag.
61. The squeezing makes it almost dry.
62. He winds it.
63. The winding is around his index finger.
64. The winding is in loops.
65. The loops are tight.

66. He scoops a crescent of wax.
67. The scooping is with his fingercloth.
68. He strokes the wax.
69. The stroking is against the leather.

70. The shine begins to come.
71. It moves up through the film.
72. It reflects the lights.
73. The lights are neon.

74. He reaches for a can.
75. The can is wax.
76. The wax is clear.
77. The wax is the touch.
78. The touch is for finishing.
79. The touch is to the job.

80. His fingercloth rubs the wax.
81. The rubbing is in circles.
82. The rubbing is slow.
83. His fingercloth caresses the shoes.

84. The Boy unwinds his fingercloth.
85. He eyes the shine.
86. His look is glazed.
87. His look is bored.

88. He finds a cloth.
89. The cloth is in his hip pocket.
90. The cloth is for finishing.
91. The cloth is soft.
92. The cloth is stained.
93. The stain is from polish.
94. The polish is from other shoes.
95. The shoes belonged to other travelers.

96. He flicks the cloth.
97. The flicking is across the shoes.
98. The flicking is around them.
99. The flicking is over them.
100. The flicking whips the shine to attention.

101. His hands are nervous.
102. They are long-fingered.
103. They make the cloth pop.
104. They make the cloth crackle.
105. They coax the shine.

106. He steps back.
107. The stepping is sudden.
108. His head is down.
109. One hand reaches for his change.
110. He readies himself.

111. He does not look at the crispness.
112. The crispness is the shine.
113. The shine is bright.

114. The traveler descends from his throne.
115. The throne is kingly.
116. He fishes for his wallet.
117. He tries to look important.
118. He tries to look worldly.

119. The Boy waits.
120. His face is unsmiling.
121. His face is without emotion.

122. Payment is met with a stare.
123. Payment is without a tip.
124. The stare is half-surly.
125. The stare is disgusted.
126. The stare is meant to be insulting.

127. A tip is met with a smile.
128. A tip is met with a wink.
129. A tip is met with a "Thank you, sir."
130. The smile fades as the traveler turns.
131. The traveler retreats.
132. The retreat is to the lobby.
133. The lobby is in the airport.

134. And the Boy readies himself.
135. The readiness is for more shoes.

☞ SUGGESTION: Write about a monotonous job you have had to do. Or write about the idea that all work, no matter how menial, is dignified. Or write about the kind of meaningful work you hope to do.

Bioscope Feedback

1. Man has been experimenting.
2. The experimentation has been for centuries.
3. The experiments are in meditation.
4. The experiments are in self-hypnosis.
5. The experiments are in Yoga.
6. The experiments are in Zen.
7. Their purpose is to help man.
8. The help is to "turn on."
9. The "turning on" occurs naturally.
10. The "turning on" is turning energy.
11. The turning is inward.

12. Masters achieve states.
13. The states are trancelike.
14. The states are serene.
15. The states provide satisfaction.
16. The satisfaction is great.
17. The states provide clarity.
18. The clarity is psychic.

19. Feedback is an answer.
20. The feedback is bioscope.
21. The answer is possible.
22. The answer is contemporary.
23. The answer is to a question.
24. The question is old.
25. The question concerns methods.
26. The methods are for meditation.

27. A bioscope is a machine.
28. The machine monitors waves.
29. The waves are in the brain.
30. Monitoring occurs through sensors.
31. The sensors are electrodes.
32. The sensors are taped.
33. The taping is to the skull.

34. A "picture" is shown.
35. The picture is of waves.
36. The waves are in the brain.
37. The showing is on a screen.
38. The picture provides information.
39. The information is about activity.
40. The activity is the brain's.

41. One wave provides a feeling.
42. The wave is called "Alpha."
43. The feeling is tranquillity.
44. The feeling is associated.
45. The association is with states.
46. The states are meditative.

47. The machine rewards the individual.
48. The reward is a beep.
49. The reward is for producing waves.
50. The waves are "Alpha."

51. The signals come through clearing.
52. The clearing is of one's mind.

53. The clearing is accomplished.
54. The accomplishment is letting go.
55. The accomplishment is not straining.
56. The accomplishment is alertness.
57. The alertness is passive.

58. The beep provides feedback.
59. The individual gets feedback.
60. Feedback concerns production.
61. Alpha waves are produced.
62. Feedback helps the individual.
63. The help is to develop strength.
64. The strength is in meditation.

65. Thus the bioscope may become a tool.
66. The tool would be for meditation.
67. The tool would be for self-knowledge.
68. The tool would be in the future.
69. The future is not distant.

☞ SUGGESTION: Science fiction writers frequently describe machines that control people's minds. Does the bioscope sound like a mind-control machine? What kind of laws might be necessary to supervise the manufacture and use of the bioscope? What might be some of the dangers as well as some of the advantages?

Ski Dreamer

1. It was early.
2. It was Saturday.
3. It was morning.
4. It was in the dead of winter.

5. The car was black.
6. The car was low slung.
7. The car was a fastback.
8. The car had skis strapped on.
9. The strapping was on the back.
10. The car screamed out of the darkness.
11. The car screamed down the highway.

12. The man was inside the car.
13. The man eyed the ridges.
14. The ridges were snow-covered.
15. The ridges were off to the east.

16. There the sky was slate gray.
17. The sky was frothed with clouds.
18. The clouds were thin.

19. Poles flicked by.
20. The poles were for telephone lines.

21. He listened to the whir.
22. The whir was of the car heater.
23. The whir was soft.
24. The whir was rhythmic.

*25. He stared at the mountains.
26. The mountains were jagged.
27. The mountains lifted from the plain.
28. The plain was monotonous.

29. He thought about the slopes.
30. The slopes were powdered.
31. The powder was snow.
32. The snow was fresh.

* You may want to combine sentences 21–24 and 25–28.

33. His mind pictured the lodge.
34. The lodge was steep-roofed.
35. The lodge nestled in the shadows.
36. The shadows were made by the mountain.
37. The shadows were chill.

*38. Skiers would be standing around the lodge.
39. They would be watching the sun come up.
40. The sun came up over the mountain's face.
41. The mountain's face was steep.

42. Then the diesel engines would start up.
43. The engines were for the chairlift.

44. The first skiers would angle down the mountain.
45. They would traverse back and forth.
46. The traversing was across the slope.
47. The traversing was through a crust.
48. The crust was of powder.

49. Puffs would follow their turns.
50. The puffs were of snow.
51. The puffs were glittering.
52. The turns were swooping.
53. The turns were birdlike.

54. The man smiled.
55. The man thought about the mountain.
56. The man thought about the day ahead.
57. The day would be full of freedom.

58. He imagined the feel.
59. The feel was of buckles.
60. The buckles snapped.
61. The feel was of bindings.
62. The bindings clicked on his boots.
63. The feel was of wind.
64. The wind laced his cheeks.
65. The wind bit his ears.
66. The feel was of snow.
67. The snow slid under his skis.
68. The snow crunched.
69. The snow squeaked.

70. He thought about himself.
71. He would be poised.
72. He would be near the top of the mountain.
73. He would be ready for his first run.

74. He would take a breath.
75. The breath would be deep.
76. The breath would fill his lungs.
77. He would flex his knees.

78. The snow would be grainy.
79. The snow would be crystalline.

80. His stomach would tense.

81. And then he would push off.
82. His skis would break loose.
83. The breaking loose would force him to crouch.
84. His weight would be forward.

85. There would be the click.
86. There would be the chatter.
87. The chatter would be of skis.
88. The chatter would be as he came out of the turn.
89. The turn would be the first one.

90. His body would dip.
91. His body would sway.
92. The sway would be from rhythms.
93. The rhythms would be from skiing.
94. His knees would flex.
95. The flexing would be with the bumps.
96. The flexing would be with the turns.

97. His motions would be smooth.
98. His motions would be controlled.

99. It would be good.
100. The good was to let go.

* Notice that from here on the man is thinking about what *will* happen, not what has happened. Your combined sentences will have to show that difference.

☞ SUGGESTION: Is there something you like to think about doing? See it again, clear in your mind's eye. Then write it down so your readers can see it as clearly as you do.

The Black Death

1. Man has always been fearful.
2. His fear is of the unknown.
3. His fear is of things.
4. The things cannot be understood.

5. It is difficult.
6. The difficulty is in estimation.
7. The estimation is of fear.
8. The fear accompanied the plagues.
9. The plagues were widespread.
10. The plagues were bubonic.
11. The plagues were during medieval times.
12. The plagues were during the Renaissance.
13. The plagues were during the nineteenth century.

14. The plague had a cause.
15. The cause was not understood until 1894.
16. The cause was confirmed in 1908.

17. It was only then that man understood.
18. The understanding was that the disease was carried.
19. Fleas were the carriers.
20. The fleas lived on rats.
21. The fleas lived on other rodents.

22. The disease was called the Black Death.
23. The calling was during the Middle Ages.
24. The calling was because of the disease's effects.
25. The effects were on the body.
26. The body was human.

27. Fever marked the Black Death.
28. Chills marked the Black Death.
29. Swelling marked the Black Death.
30. The swelling was severe.
31. The swelling was of the lymph nodes.
32. The nodes were in the groin.
33. The nodes were in other parts.
34. The parts were in the body.

35. The disease was accompanied by hemorrhages.
36. The hemorrhages made dark spots.
37. The spots were on the skin.
38. The disease was accompanied by a rate.
39. The rate was of death.
40. The rate was extremely high.

41. Historians estimate it killed people.
42. The people were hundreds of thousands.
43. The people were in Europe.
44. The people were in England.
45. The killing was during the fourteenth century.

46. The Black Death broke out again.
47. The breaking out was during the seventeenth century.
48. Populations were ravaged.

49. Lyon lost half of its population.
50. The loss was in 1628.
51. Milan lost 86,000 persons.
52. The Venetian Republic lost 500,000.

53. The plague also swept the continent.
54. The sweep was during the eighteenth century.
55. 300,000 died in Austria.
56. 215,000 died in Brandenburg.

57. The epidemic claimed 60,000.
58. The claim was in Moscow.
59. The claim was in 1771.

60. The outbreak occurred during the last years.
61. This was the last outbreak.
62. The years were in the nineteenth century.
63. The outbreak was major.
64. The outbreak was in China.

65. The plague was carried far.
66. The plague was carried wide.
67. The plague was carried by vessels.
68. The vessels were ocean going.

69. The plague was diagnosed.
70. The diagnosis was made in the United States.
71. The diagnosis was in 1902.
72. The diagnosis was in San Francisco.

73. Now the fleas have spread.
74. The fleas are infected.
75. The fleas were imported from China.
76. The spreading is over the western part.
77. The part is of the United States.
78. The spreading is into Canada.

79. The fleas are now carried by thirty-eight rodents.
80. The rodents are wild.
81. The rodents include rats.
82. The rodents include squirrels.
83. The rodents include prairie dogs.
84. The rodents include rabbits.
85. The rodents include meadow mice.

86. Control is now exercised.
87. The control is of rodents.
88. The exercise is in areas.
89. The areas are of epidemics.
90. The epidemics are potential.
91. The areas are especially the cities.

92. DDT has been used.
93. The use is to control the population.
94. The population is fleas.
95. But DDT has side effects.
96. The side effects are unfortunate.
97. The side effects damage life.
98. The life is human.
99. The side effects damage the environment.

100. So the Black Death is still with us.
101. The Black Death is a legacy.
102. The legacy is from the past.
103. But now the Black Death is understood.
104. The Black Death seems less frightening.

Intergalaxy Report

1. The Council was convened.
2. The convening occurred at 22:11.
3. 22:11 was Sixth Dimension Time.

4. A Time Probe had just returned.
5. The return was from a mission.
6. The mission was into a galaxy.
7. The galaxy was being charted.
8. The charting was through a series.
9. The series was of probes.

10. All Thought Channels were cleared.
11. The clearing was for broadcast.
12. The broadcast was a report.
13. The report would be of interest.
14. The interest would be extreme.
15. The interest would be to citizens.
16. The citizens belonged to the galaxy.

17. The report was filed at 22:12.
18. The report was filed by the commander.
19. The report was in accordance with specifications.
20. The specifications were intergalactic.

21. The report follows here.
22. The following is as it was broadcast.
23. The report has not been changed.

THE REPORT

24. The patrol set down.
25. The place was Planet 4982015-12-E.

26. Inhabitants swarmed.
27. The swarming was at a distance.
28. The distance was from a spot.
29. The spot was where we emerged.
30. The emerging was from the Time Probe.

31. We were unnoticed.
32. The unnoticing was by inhabitants.
33. Inhabitants did not question us.
34. Inhabitants did not detain us.

35. We entered the Probe Area.
36. The entry was on schedule.
37. The entry was according to plans.
38. The plans had been designed earlier.
39. The chief made the plans.

40. The area was called a center.
41. The center was for shopping.

42. Here we noted behaviors.
43. The behaviors are strange.
44. The behaviors are demonstrated.
45. The demonstration is by the inhabitants.

46. Women come in hordes.
47. The hordes are great.
48. The hordes are jabbering.
49. The women pull children.
50. The pulling is along behind.

51. Women clog the aisles.
52. Women clamor over the merchandise.
53. The merchandise is spread out.
54. The merchandise is for handling.
55. The women are like ants.
56. The ants are on a pile.
57. The pile is made of sugar.

58. Overhead are the faces.
59. The faces are of the managers.
60. The faces survey the scene below.
61. The scene is tense.
62. The managers have created the scene.
63. The creation comes from years of experience.

64. The mob moves through a section.
65. The section is ready to wear.
66. The ready to wear is for children.
67. The mob moves around the shoes.
68. The mob moves past the toys.
69. The mob moves toward a heap.
70. The heap is of blouses.

71. Girls linger at a counter.
72. The girls are young.
73. The counter is for cosmetics.
74. The girls comb their hair.
75. The girls smile.
76. The smiling is into mirrors.

77. Women finger pans.
78. The pans are for cooking.
79. The women are fat.
80. The women are middle-aged.
81. The women have their hair in curlers.

82. Men inspect furniture.
83. The men are fat.
84. The men are middle-aged.
85. The men smoke cigars.
86. The furniture is vinyl.
87. The furniture is aluminum.
88. The furniture is for lawns.

89. Everything is packaged.
90. Everything is ready to go.
91. Everything is imitation.
92. Everything is cheaply made.
93. Everything is discounted.

94. The inhabitants buy.
95. The buying is impulsive.
96. The inhabitants scramble.
97. The scrambling is for things.
98. The inhabitants push each other.
99. The pushing is out of the way.

100. Music dribbles down the wall.
101. The music is from loudspeakers.
102. The music is soapy.
103. The music bathes the mob.
104. The bathing is in a suggestion.
105. The suggestion is about bills.
106. Bills never come due.

107. A voice barks.
108. The barking is at the crowd.
109. The barking is every minute or two.
110. The barking announces "super specials."

111. The inhabitants move with each bark.
112. The inhabitants flow toward the place.
113. The place is where the "specials" are.

114. A message is repeated.
115. The repeating is everywhere.
116. The repeating is relentless.
117. The message is about consuming.
118. Consuming is a good thing.

119. Consuming makes for happiness.
120. Consuming makes for contentment.
121. Consuming makes for pleasure.

122. The inhabitants believe the message.
123. The message has been programmed.
124. The programming is into their minds.
125. The programming has been going on for years.
126. The inhabitants respond.
127. The inhabitants fill the shopping carts.

128. Their faces are slack-eyed.
129. Their faces are unthinking.

130. Buying is the way of life.
131. The way is for the inhabitants.
132. The inhabitants are on this planet.

133. We conclude this report.
134. Our conclusion is a suggestion.
135. No further probes should be sent.
136. The sending would be to this planet.

☞ SUGGESTION: Ask yourself whether this is a fair or objective report of shopping centers as you know them. Make a list of words that seem to reveal the probe's point of view or attitude toward what they see and hear. How does this list influence you as a reader? Then try making a similar report of some place you visit regularly enough that you can be specific about it. In your report, act as if you are seeing the situation for the first time, as the Time Probe might see it if they were to make another visit. Try to use words that will influence your readers to see it as you do.

Walking on the Moon

1. What does it mean to walk on the moon?

2. It means we possess an ability.
3. The ability is extraordinary.
4. The ability is to set goals.
5. The ability is to begin programs.
6. The programs are for research.
7. The programs are for training.
8. The ability is to coordinate efforts.
9. The efforts are of agencies.
10. The agencies are in government.
11. The agencies are in the military.
12. The agencies are in business.

13. It means that we possess the know-how.
14. The know-how is technical.
15. The know-how is to build rockets.
16. The know-how is to build systems.
17. The systems are electronic.
18. The systems can be monitored by computers.
19. The computers are for guidance.
20. The rockets are guided.

21. It means that we have people.
22. The people are adventurous.
23. The people are highly trained.
24. They are willing to pioneer.
25. The pioneering is into the frontiers.
26. The frontiers include medicine.
27. The frontiers include meteorology.
28. The frontiers include electronics.
29. The frontiers include communications.
30. The frontiers include data retrieval.
31. The frontiers include photography.
32. The frontiers include thermodynamics.
33. The frontiers include engineering.
34. The frontiers include navigation.
35. The frontiers include a host of other fields.

36. It means that we have committed dollars.
37. The dollars are billions.
38. The commitment is toward an objective.
39. The objective is single.
40. The objective is walking on the moon.

41. Many people are now asking another question.
42. The question is important.
43. The importance is real.
44. The importance is philosophical.
45. Can we organize ourselves?
46. The organization would be to solve our problems.
47. The problems are social.

48. Some people answer yes.
49. The answer is that we have the know-how.
50. All we need is the commitment.
51. The commitment is financial.
52. The commitment comes from the government.
53. The commitment would enable us.
54. The enabling would be to solve problems.
55. The solving would be systematic.
56. The solving would be efficient.

57. Others answer no.
58. They say that we can solve some problems.
59. These problems are technical.
60. These problems are mechanical.
61. These problems are the ones of getting to the moon.
62. But we cannot solve other problems.
63. The other problems are social.
64. The other problems are cultural.

☞ SUGGESTION: Identify a single, specific problem that you think can—and should—be solved immediately. Make a case for why this problem must receive immediate attention.

phase two

introduction

In Phase I you've been experimenting—exploring transforms on your own, making combinations that sound right to you. You've been developing a feel for the patterns of written English. In Phase II you'll be making slightly different explorations. Here you'll be given a model sentence that has been broken down into levels so you can see the way the sentence is built. Then you'll imitate this model as you perform your own transforms.

The explorations you make here, like those in Phase I, will build on things you already know. You won't be doing anything much different, or much harder, than what you did in Phase I. The difference is that this time you'll be deliberately copying a definite pattern. You'll be getting practice in what Francis Christensen calls "the cumulative sentence," a kind of sentence that is frequently used by skillful professional writers.[1]

Probably the easiest way to understand what these levels are and how they work is to begin with a group of kernels and see how they fit together:

Harold shuffled to the front of the room.
Harold knotted his shoulders.
Harold jammed his hands into his pockets.

One way of combining these kernels will give us:

Harold shuffled to the front of the room, knotting his shoulders and jamming his hands into his pockets.

What has happened here is that we have picked the first kernel as being the most important—*Harold shuffled to the front of the room*—and used it as the *base clause* in the transform. The other two kernels have been pushed down to a *second level*. And we can tell that they are both on the same level because they pattern alike:

knot*ting* his shoulders,
jamm*ing* his hands into his pockets.

[1] Francis Christensen, *Notes Toward a New Rhetoric: Six Essays for Teachers* (New York: Harper & Row, 1967).

So you can see more easily what the pattern is, the base clause is italicized and numbered (1); the second level modifiers are numbered (2):

(1) *Harold shuffled to the front of the room,*
    (2) knotting his shoulders,
    (2) jamming his hands into his pockets.

If we want to, we can add more -*ing* phrases. It will still be a two-level sentence, because all the second-level parts are built alike:

(1) *Harold shuffled to the front of the room,*
    (2) knotting his shoulders,
    (2) jamming his hands into his pockets,
    (2) scowling at the blackboard,
    (2) muttering to himself.

Even though we change the order of the kernels, the sentence remains two level as long as the second-level kernels keep the same pattern:

    (2) Muttering to himself,
(1) *Harold shuffled to the front of the room,*
    (2) jamming his hands into his pockets,
    (2) knotting his shoulders,
    (2) scowling at the blackboard.

Just as the base clause can come anywhere in the combined sentence, so the second-level modifiers can come in different forms; they don't have to begin with -*ing* words. Here is a two-level transform that uses a somewhat different pattern:

Harold shuffled to the front of the room.
Harold was tired from the night before.
Harold was bored with the discussion.
Harold was annoyed with the teacher.

When we combine these kernels, we can get:

(1) *Harold shuffled to the front of the room,*
    (2) tired from the night before,
    (2) bored with the discussion, and
    (2) annoyed with the teacher.

We dropped "Harold was" and began all the second-level modifiers with -*ed* words, thus getting another two-level sentence.

We could get still another pattern if we went back to the original kernels and used a different kind of transform:

Harold shuffled to the front of the room.
Harold knotted his shoulders.
Harold jammed his hands into his pockets.

Instead of beginning the second-level modifiers with *-ing* words, we can start with nouns:

(1) *Harold shuffled to the front of the room,*
    (2) his shoulder knotted,
    (2) his hands jammed into his pockets.

The second-level modifiers here are *almost* sentences—they are missing only one word:

His shoulders [were] knotted.
His hands [were] jammed into his pockets.

Transforms like this, where the change involves dropping a part of the verb, are called *absolutes*; the name, however, isn't important. What matters is that you get a sense of the pattern and understand what happens when you make the transform.

Sometimes kernels can be combined so that not all the modifiers follow the same pattern. When this happens, we get a *multilevel* sentence[2]:

Harold jammed his hands into his pockets.
Harold shuffled to the front of the room.
Harold was bored with the discussion.
Harold was annoyed with the teacher.

    (2) His hands jammed into his pockets,

---

[2] The numbering system used here is different from the one suggested by Christensen in his *Notes Toward a New Rhetoric*. Christensen uses (2) after the base clause, even if the number (2) has already been used before the base clause, and even if the modifiers are not parallel. According to Christensen, "His hands jammed into his pockets, Harold shuffled to the front of the room, bored with the discussion and annoyed with the teacher," would be numbered (2), (1), (2), (2). Because students often find the duplicate (2)'s confusing, a continuous numbering system is used throughout this text; the only time a number is repeated is when the modifiers are actually parallel in form. After all, how the levels are numbered, or whether they are numbered at all, is less important than seeing how the parts interlock.

(1) *Harold shuffled to the front of the room,*
        (3) bored with the discussion, and
        (3) annoyed with the teacher.

This sentence has three levels because the pattern used in (2)—*hands jammed into his pockets*—is different from the pattern in (3)—*bored and annoyed*.

    Sometimes we make transforms where the patterns are even more complicated.

Harold jammed his hands into his pockets.
Harold shuffled to the front of the room.
Harold was tired from the night before.
Harold was bored with the discussion.
Harold scowled at the teacher.
The teacher returned the scowl.

We can combine these kernels so that we get a five-level sentence, but because the parts fit together smoothly the result doesn't *seem* complicated:

      (2) His hands jammed into his pockets,
(1) *Harold shuffled to the front of the room,*
        (3) tired from the night before,
        (3) bored with the discussion,
           (4) scowling at the teacher,
               (5) who returned his scowl.

    And sometimes we can combine a group of kernels in such a way that we get two *base* clauses. When this happens, we count the levels for each base clause separately, just as though they were not joined together:

and
     Harold shuffled to the front of the room.
     Harold scowled at the teacher.
     The teacher returned the scowl.
     The other students sat quietly.
The other students waited for the explosion.

(1) *Harold shuffled to the front of the room,*
    (2) scowling at the teacher,
        (3) who returned his scowl, and
(1) *the other students sat quietly,*
    (2) waiting for the explosion.

Here *Harold shuffled to the front of the room* and *the other students sat quietly* are both numbered (1) because they are both base clauses.

Whether the transforms have one base clause or more than one, whether they come in two levels or more than two, the pieces always lock together according to regular patterns. This interlocking process is extremely systematic. Although you (and everybody else who writes English) can make an infinite number of different sentences, all saying an infinite number of different things, the *patterns* you use will be repeated over and over. Once you have become comfortable in using these patterns, you can put together cumulative sentences without consciously thinking about the patterns you use. Almost automatically you'll select as your base clause the thing you want to emphasize, and you'll attach second-level and third-level modifiers easily and naturally. The purpose of Phase II is to help you develop that ease.

One way of becoming comfortable with the patterns available in English is to use them deliberately, to follow certain models over and over again. The models given here are not necessarily any better than some of the sentences you've been writing; the "goodness" of a sentence depends on where it's used and what it's used for. The models are provided simply to help you do things with language that you may not have done before, and to offer you options you may not have realized you had.

how to use phase two

1. First, study the model sentence, reading it aloud several times so that you can hear the rhythm and fix the pattern in your mind.
2. Next, look at the kernel sentences, seeing how you can fit them together with the italicized kernel as the base clause.
3. Then transform the kernels to create a new sentence that is built like the model but not necessarily identical to it.
4. After you've practiced transforming the kernels into sentences that pattern like the model, you can put the book aside and make your own sentences, following the same general pattern. You'll be surprised at how easy it is, and pleased with the variety it gives to your writing.

EXPLORATIONS

MODEL A: Sentence in Two Levels

MODEL

---

1. *The driver wheeled his van.*
2. The wheeling was into the lot.
3. The lot was for trucks.
4. The driver squinted against the sun.
5. The sun was afternoon.
6. The driver checked his mirror.
7. The mirror was rearview.

(1) *The driver wheeled his van into the truck lot,*
   (2) squinting against the afternoon sun,
   (2) checking his rearview mirror.

Now make your own transforms, following the model:

1. *The present moment is electric.*
2. The present moment sparks with life.
3. The present moment crackles with possibilities.
4. The possibilities are untried.

1. *The life of Robert Kennedy was like a bridge.*
2. The life of Robert Kennedy spanned the country.
3. The life of Robert Kennedy rose above the landscape.
4. The life of Robert Kennedy connected people.
5. The life of Robert Kennedy connected ideas.

1. *The go-go dancer stared at the window.*
2. The go-go dancer was bird-faced.
3. The go-go dancer was thin.
4. The window was rain-smeared.
5. The go-go dancer watched the rain.
6. The go-go dancer thought about her boy friend.
7. The boy friend was in the front row.

1. *The player took the handoff.*
2. The handoff was from the quarterback.
3. The player turned sharply.
4. The player dropped one shoulder.

5. The dropping was in a fake.
6. The fake was exaggerated.
7. The player rolled against the tide.
8. The tide was of tacklers.

1. *The shouts echoed.*
2. The shouts were shrill.
3. The shouts were discordant.
4. The shouts sounded full of pain.
5. The pain was human.
6. The shouts felt tense.
7. The tenseness was with hostility.

1. *The worker is on the run.*
2. The worker is average.
3. The worker lifts.
4. The worker pushes.
5. The worker strains.
6. The straining is to make a better living.
7. The worker battles.
8. The battling is against inflation.
9. The worker tries.
10. The trying is to maintain a standard.
11. The standard is respectable.
12. The standard is of living.

1. *Ecology is an issue.*
2. The issue is political.
3. The issue is hot.
4. The issue takes up time in all campaigns.
5. The issue gets lip service.
6. The lip service is from all candidates.
7. The issue is being exploited.
8. The exploitation is to get votes.

1. *The job seeker comes in.*
2. The job seeker is nervous.
3. The job seeker is blinking.
4. The blinking is with embarrassment.
5. The job seeker is fumbling.
6. The fumbling is for words.

MODEL B: Sentence in Two Levels with the Base Clause in the Middle

---

MODEL

---

1. The teacher smiled to himself.
2. *The teacher erased the blackboard.*
3. The erasing was with a sweep.
4. The sweep was lazy.
5. The teacher trailed patterns.
6. The patterns were of chalkdust.
7. The chalkdust was gritty.
8. The chalkdust was grayish.

    (2) Smiling to himself,
(1) *the teacher erased the blackboard with a lazy sweep,*
    (2) trailing patterns of gritty, grayish chalkdust.

Now make your own transforms, following the model:

1. The car careened out of the lot.
2. *The car rumbled down the alley.*
3. The alley was bricked in.
4. The alley was deserted.
5. The car weaved from side to side.

1. Mark hoped to catch a quick nap.
2. *Mark slumped into his desk.*
3. Mark closed his eyes.
4. Mark let sleep gather him in.
5. The gathering was soft.

1. The storm waves broke.
2. The breaking was in great swells.
3. *The storm waves thundered against the rocks.*
4. The storm waves exploded into foam.
5. The storm waves spewed white.
6. The spewing was high up the cliffs.
7. The cliffs were encrusted with barnacles.

1. The housewife heard creaks.
2. The creaks were strange.
3. *The housewife listened to the noises.*
4. The noises were in the house.
5. The housewife felt her pulse quicken.

1. Power lines run parallel to the road.
2. *Power lines stretch through the desert.*
3. Power lines span gulches.
4. Power lines span streambeds.
5. The streambeds are alkali.
6. Power lines loop from pole to pole.
7. Power lines stretch electricity.
8. The stretching is from town to town.

1. We look at Southeast Asia.
2. *We examine the problem.*
3. We try to find an answer.
4. We struggle with options.
5. We look for solutions.
6. The solutions will be workable.

MODEL C: Sentence in Two Levels with Absolutes

MODEL

---

1. The center's legs were stiff.
2. The center's legs were muscled.
3. *The center went up for the ball.*
4. The center was tall.
5. The center was black.
6. The center's arms were extended.
7. The center's arms were long.
8. The center's elbows were out.
9. The center's hands reached.

   (2) Legs stiff and muscled,
(1) *the tall black center went up for the ball,*
   (2) his long arms extended,
   (2) his elbows out,
   (2) his hands reaching.

Now make your own transforms, following the model:

1. *The skier came over a crest.*
2. The crest was choppy.
3. The crest was low.
4. The skier's body was crouched.
5. The skier's weight was forward.
6. One ski was slightly ahead of the other.

1. *Rock music burst out of the speakers.*
2. The sounds were loud.
3. The sounds were harsh.
4. The rhythms were primitive.

1. Molly's eyes were blank.
2. *Molly fingered the bill.*
3. The bill was for the telephone.
4. The fingering was with disgust.
5. Molly's thumb traced the figures.
6. Molly's palm smoothed the paper.

1. *Two girls elbow into line.*
2. Their legs are long.
3. Their skirts are short.
4. Their talk is slangy.
5. Their talk is bright.

1. The flag is a piece of cloth.
2. The piece of cloth provides a focus.
3. The focus is for ceremonies.
4. *The flag is a symbol.*
5. The flag's presence helps to unite a people.
6. The unification is for a moment or two.

1. *The lecture hall was a waiting room.*
2. The waiting room was institutional.
3. Its walls were decorated.
4. The decorating was in mustard green.
5. Its aisles were crowded.
6. The crowding was with chairs.
7. The chairs were scarred.
8. Its interior was stuffed.
9. The stuffing was with bodies.
10. The bodies sweated.
11. Its appearance mirrored the philosophy.
12. The philosophy was of the system.
13. The system was welfare.

MODEL D: Multilevel Sentence

MODEL

1. *The wingman hurtled down the ice.*
2. The wingman was lean.
3. The wingman was raw-boned.
4. The ice was bright.
5. His skates flashed.
6. The puck was cradled by his stick.
7. He forced the goalie.
8. The goalie came out.
9. The goalie tried to stop him.

  (1) *The lean, raw-boned wingman hurtled down the bright ice,*
    (2) his skates flashing,
    (2) the puck cradled by his stick,
      (3) forcing the goalie to come out and try to stop him.

Now make your own transforms. Notice, however, that from now on the patterns you come up with probably won't be exactly like the model. Your transformed sentences should all have more than two levels, but they will not necessarily begin with absolutes, nor will the third level necessarily begin with an *-ing* word.

1. *The cat came with a leap.*
2. The cat was tan.
3. The cat was tawny.
4. The cat's body was coiled.
5. The cat sprang on its prey.

1. *The election results will come in slowly.*
2. The precincts report first.
3. The precincts are small.
4. The precincts provide data.
5. The data are for predictions.
6. The predictions are broadcasted.
7. The broadcasting is nationwide.

1. *A carburetor is located.*
2. The location is on top of the engine.
3. A carburetor serves to mix gasoline.
4. The gasoline is mixed with air.
5. The fuel becomes atomized.
6. The fuel becomes ready.
7. The readiness is for combustion.

1. *Joel's father goes to sleep.*
2. He sleeps after dinner.
3. His head is on the floor.
4. The floor is bare.
5. His feet are on the sofa.
6. His feet are stockinged.
7. The sofa is a couch.
8. The couch is kept for the man.
9. The keeping is special.
10. The man is old.
11. The couch is to prop his feet on.

1. *Children begin school.*
2. The children are eager.
3. The eagerness is with enthusiasm.
4. The eagerness is for an experience.
5. The experience is new.
6. The children are anxious.
7. The anxiousness is to enter a world.
8. The world is of knowledge.
9. The world is inhabited.
10. Its inhabitants are adults.
11. The adults possess an authority.
12. The authority is mysterious.

1. *Repairing a machine can be simple.*
2. The machine is for sewing.
3. The machine has a treadle.
4. The machine is old.
5. Repairing is a matter.
6. The matter is of replacing a belt.
7. The belt is leather.
8. The belt stretches from the drive wheel.
9. The belt stretches to a gear.

10. The gear is attached to the treadle.
11. The matter is adjusting the tension.

1. *Reports show something.*
2. Many children go to bed.
3. The children are American.
4. The children are hungry at bedtime.
5. Their legs are thin.
6. Their arms are thin.
7. The thinness is painful.
8. Their bellies are distended.
9. Their bellies are unfilled.
10. The children lack protein.
11. Protein comes in the form.
12. The form is meat.
13. The form is grain.
14. Farmers are paid not to grow meat.
15. Farmers are paid not to grow grain.

MODEL E: Multilevel Sentence with the Base Clause in the Middle

---

MODEL

---

1. The stew attracted the whole family.
2. The attraction was by its smell.
3. *The stew bubbled.*
4. The bubbling was in the pot.
5. The carrots were crisp.
6. The carrots were colorful.
7. The chunks of meat were rich.
8. The chunks of meat were brown.

   (2) Attracting the whole family by its smell,
(1) *the stew bubbled in the pot,*
      (3) the carrots crisp and colorful,
      (3) the chunks of meat rich and brown.

Now make your own transforms. Remember the patterns you come up with probably won't be exactly like the model. Your transformed sentences will not all begin with -*ing* words, nor will the third-level modifiers all be absolutes.

1. The college student is alert.
2. The college student is aggressive.
3. The college student is well trained.
4. *The college student searches for answers.*
5. The college student is modern.
6. The college student probes beneath the surface.
7. The college student seeks truth.
8. The truth is hidden.

1. The motorcycle throbbed heavily.
2. *The motorcycle idled at the stoplight.*
3. The motorcycle was lean.
4. The motorcycle was stripped.
5. The stripping was of its weight.
6. The motorcycle was poised.
7. The poising was for acceleration.

1. Many Vista workers are excited.
2. Vista workers are excited by social action.
3. *Many Vista workers are on the job.*
4. Vista workers help others.
5. Vista workers organize the community.
6. Vista workers make the world more livable.

1. Railroad passenger service is outdated by aircraft.
2. Railroad passenger service is expensive to operate.
3. *Railroad passenger service must work hard for changes.*
4. Railroad passenger service must improve its coaches.
5. Railroad passenger service must serve good food.
6. Railroad passenger service must revise schedules.
7. Railroad passenger service must treat customers courteously.

1. The willows dipped.
2. The willows danced at the wind's bidding.
3. *The willows swayed.*
4. Their branches were outlined against the sky.
5. Their branches were trailing.

1. SAC is armed.
2. SAC is ready.
3. *SAC is on twenty-four-hour alert.*
4. SAC has planes.
5. The planes are lined up.
6. SAC has pilots.
7. The pilots are directed.
8. The direction is toward their targets.
9. SAC has backup systems.
10. The backup systems are in order.

MODEL F: Sentence with Two Base Clauses and Two Levels

MODEL

> 1. A band grinned at the tourists.
> 2. The band was small.
> 3. *The band settled in.*
> 4. The band was of construction workers.
> and   5. The band winked.
> then   6. The band swaggered back and forth.
> 7. The band waited for the action.
> 8. *The police came.*
> 9. The police had handcuffs.
> 10. The handcuffs were ready.

    (2) Grinning at the tourists,
(1) *a small band of construction workers settled in,*
    (2) winking,
    (2) swaggering back and forth,
    (2) waiting for the action,
(1) *and then the police came,*
    (2) their handcuffs ready.

Now make your own transforms, following the general patterns of the model:

```
      ┌── 1. The music was loud.
and      2. The music was glittering with guitars.
      └── 3. The dancers moved with the sound.
          4. Their bodies were jerking.
          5. Their hips were grinding.
          6. Their hips were gyrating.
          7. Their feet were pawing the floor.
```

```
      ┌── 1. Smog hung over the city.
         2. Smog choked off the light.
and      3. The light was from the sun.
      └── 4. All the heat seemed trapped.
          5. The heat mixed with dirt.
          6. The heat mixed with waste.
          7. The waste was industrial.
          8. The heat made the air unbearable.
```

```
          1. Some students bow.
          2. Some students scrape.
      ┌── 3. Some students march through the system.
         4. Some students are docile.
and      5. Some students are cow-eyed.
      └── 6. The system finally "educates" them.
          7. The system helps them to "adjust."
          8. The system encourages them to "fit in."
          9. The system encourages them not to ask questions.
         10. The questions are about the Establishment.
```

```
      ┌── 1. A beard keeps one's face warm.
         2. A beard protects one's face.
but      3. The protection is from the cold.
also     4. A beard shields one's face.
         5. The shielding is from the wind.
      └── 6. A beard attracts attention.
          7. A beard gives people something.
          8. The something is to talk about.
          9. A beard makes one's ideas noticed.
```

      ┌─ **1.** *Many of Sutton's poems are dead.*
      │   **2.** His lines are buried in geography.
but │   **3.** His words are muffled in cliché.
      └─ **4.** *This poem is alive.*
          5. This poem engages the reader.
          6. This poem forcing the reader to listen.
          7. This poem demands a response.

        ┌─ **1.** *The optimist sees things.*
        │   **2.** The things seem hopeful.
        │   **3.** The things seem exciting.
whereas │   **4.** The things seems rich.
        │   **5.** The richness is with promise.
        └─ **6.** *The pessimist sees things.*
           7. The things are the same.
           8. The things seem dark.
           9. The things seem impossible.
        10. The things seem hopeless.
        11. The hopelessness is absurd.

          1. The jet lifted into the horizon.
      ┌─ **2.** *The jet powered upward.*
and │   **3.** The jet was a Boeing 747.
then │   **4.** The jet trailed smoke.
      └─ **5.** *The jet banked to the east.*
          6. The jet had skin.
          7. The skin glinted.
          8. The skin was silver.
          9. The jet had shape.
        10. The shape got smaller.
        11. The jet had a roar.
        12. The roar faded.

      ┌─ **1.** *Time seemed to hang.*
      │   **2.** The hanging was motionless.
and │   **3.** The hang was teetering.
then └─ **4.** *The car edged forward.*
          5. The car had wheels.
          6. The wheels spun.
          7. The wheels caught hold.
          8. The car had an engine.

9. The engine wound up.
10. The winding was harsh.

```
        ┌── 1. *The poet works at odd hours.*
        │    2. The poet pores over books.
        │    3. The poet pores through papers.
and     │    4. The poet tries to get organized.
        │    5. The poet hopes for an idea.
        └── 6. *Sometimes the sentence happens.*
             7. The sentence is perfect.
             8. The sentence reveals a corner.
             9. The corner is of the universe.
```

```
        ┌── 1. *Children must observe the curfew.*
        │    2. The children are under fourteen.
or      │    3. Children leave the streets.
        │    4. The leaving is before 9:00 P.M.
        └── 5. *Their parents will be jailed.*
             6. The parents will be charged.
             7. The charge is child neglect.
             8. The parents are subject to fine.
```

MODEL G: Sentence with Two Base Clauses and Multilevels

```
MODEL
```

```
        ┌── 1. The children were very quiet.
        │    2. The children stared at their books.
and          3. The children had hands.
then         4. The hands were folded.
        │    5. The hands were in their laps.
        └── 6. The teacher jumped.
             7. The jumping was sudden.
             8. The jumping was to his feet.
             9. The teacher worked himself into a frenzy.
            10. The teacher's face was bright.
            11. The brightness was with rage.
            12. One hand rubbed his bottom.
            13. His bottom was tack-stung.

        (1) The children were very quiet,
            (2) staring at their books,
                (3) their hands folded in their laps,
        (1) and then the teacher suddenly jumped to his feet,
            (2) working himself into a frenzy,
                (3) his face bright with rage,
                (3)  one hand rubbing his tack-stung bottom.
```

Now make your own transforms, following the general pattern of the model:

```
          1. The diver took his leap.
      ┌── 2. The diver sprang into the air.
      │    3. The springing was high.
and        4. The diver was silhouetted against the sky.
then       5. His arms were outstretched.
      │    6. His arms came together.
      └── 7. He tucked in a roll.
           8. The roll was slow.
           9. His body was in rhythm.
          10. The rhythm was perfect.
```

11. His body plummeted down.
12. His body knifed the water.

```
       ┌── 1. *The pusher works the street.*
       │    2. The pusher is hardened.
       │    3. The pusher hustles drugs.
       │    4. The hustling is to support his habit.
and    │    5. The pusher is more afraid.
thus   │    6. The fear is of doing without.
       │    7. The pusher is less afraid.
       │    8. The fear is of being arrested.
       └── 9. *The circle widens.*
```

10. The circle is of addiction.
11. The circle engulfs the young.
12. The circle entices the gullible.

```
           1. The clouds churn with storm.
       ┌── 2. *The clouds come rolling in.*
       │    3. The clouds are sullen.
       │    4. The clouds are turbulent.
       │    5. The clouds have shapes.
and    │    6. The shapes mushroom.
       │    7. The mushrooming is against the horizon.
       └── 8. *The wind begins to build up.*
```

9. The wind brings a smell.
10. The smell is ominous.
11. The smell comes in off the water.
12. The smell tastes of salt.
13. The smell brings a memory.
14. The memory is of other storms.

```
           1. Aunt Grace hovers over the stove.
           2. Aunt Grace has hair.
           3. The hair is up in curlers.
       ┌── 4. *Aunt Grace sets out her cup.*
and    │    5. Aunt Grace measures out a teaspoonful.
then   │    6. The teaspoonful is coffee.
       │    7. The coffee is instant.
       └── 8. *Aunt Grace pours the water.*
```

9. The water has a sizzle.
10. The sizzle consumes the crystals.
11. The water fills her cup.

12. The filling is with brown.
13. The brown is melted.

  1. The shadows are outside the city.
  2. The shadows are in some place.
  3. The place is distant.
  4. *The shadows lengthen across the grass.*
  5. The shadows deepen the green.
  6. The deepening is into night.
  7. *The water trembles.*
  8. The trembling is in pools.
  9. The pools are shallow.
10. The pools are dark.
11. The water works its way.
12. The way is around the rocks.
13. The way is over the rocks.
14. The water slides in sheets.
and 15. The sheets are soft.
16. The sliding is over the lip.
17. The lip is on the waterfall.
18. *The sounds emphasize the quiet.*
19. The sounds are of evening.

  1. *Loving is such a simple matter.*
  2. The matter involves smiling.
  3. The matter involves listening.
  4. The matter involves showing concern.
  5. One hand is stretched to a person.
yet 6. The person is another.
  7. The hand offers help.
  8. *We have trouble.*
  9. The trouble is turning outward.
10. The trouble is conquering the fears.
11. The fears keep us apart.

MODEL H: Sentence Combining the Base Clauses

MODEL

1. *He turned the wheels.*
2. He pulled out on the edge.
3. The edge was banked.
and 4. The edge was of the highway.
5. He waited.
6. The waiting was for traffic to clear.
7. *He pushed on the gas.*
8. He left two autographs.
9. The autographs were black.

(1) *He turned the wheels,*
    (2) pulling out on the banked edge of the highway,
    (2) waiting for the traffic to clear,
(1) *and pushed on the gas,*
    (2) leaving two black autographs.

Now make your own transforms, following the general pattern of the model:

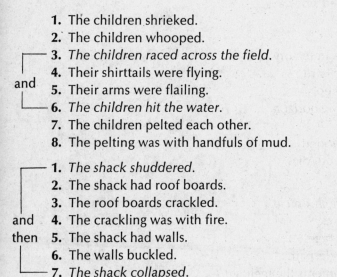

1. The children shrieked.
2. The children whooped.
3. *The children raced across the field.*
4. Their shirttails were flying.
and 5. Their arms were flailing.
6. *The children hit the water.*
7. The children pelted each other.
8. The pelting was with handfuls of mud.

1. *The shack shuddered.*
2. The shack had roof boards.
3. The roof boards crackled.
and 4. The crackling was with fire.
then 5. The shack had walls.
6. The walls buckled.
7. *The shack collapsed.*
8. The collapsing made a roar.

9. The roar was sudden.
10. The collapsing puffed up a shower.
11. The shower was from sparks.
12. The collapsing puffed up a sheet.
13. The sheet was made of flame.

1. The batter watched the pitch.
2. *The batter tensed.*
3. The batter toed the dust.

and 4. The batter dug in.
5. *The batter swung.*
6. The swinging was as hard as he could.
7. His hands squeezed the handle.
8. The handle was on the bat.
9. His weight followed his swing.

1. Grandpa's head was cocked.
2. The cocking was to one side.
3. *Grandpa listened to the news.*

and 4. Grandpa frowned.
then 5. Grandpa chewed his lip.
6. *Grandpa clicked off the radio.*
7. Grandpa sighed.
8. Grandpa swore.

1. The Frisbee is flicked sideways.
2. *The Frisbee soars.*
3. The Frisbee spins.
4. The spinning is in a trajectory.

and 5. The trajectory is upward.
6. The trajectory is steep.
7. *The Frisbee slices the horizon.*
8. The Frisbee hovers.
9. The Frisbee is cushioned.
10. The cushion is in a puddle.
11. The puddle is of air.

1. *Much literature is a chronicle.*
2. The literature is black.
3. The chronicle is of rage.
4. The chronicle is of despair.
5. The literature documents the feeling.
6. The feeling belongs to people.

7. The people are black.

and   8. The literature examines the American Dream.

9. The examination is from the underside.

10. *The literature should be familiar.*

11. All Americans should be familiar with it.

12. The familiarity should be regardless of background.

13. The background is ethnic.

1. *Senator Glump can vote for the bill.*

2. The bill is for lunches.

3. The lunches are for school.

4. Senator Glump can ignore his convictions.

5. The convictions are against charity.

or   6. Senator Glump calls it charity.

7. *Senator Glump can risk defeat.*

8. The defeat will be at the election.

9. The election will be next.

10. The defeat will be by voters.

11. The voters will be angry.

Now you are on your own. Use whichever model you think fits.

1. The gang had shoulders.
2. The shoulders were broad.
3. The shoulders were hunched.
4. *The gang huddled around the jukebox.*
5. The gang rocked with laughter.
6. The gang had voices.
7. The voices rang clear.
8. The ringing caused people to turn.
9. The ringing made people smile.

1. *The engine lumbered forward.*
2. The engine was on the train.
3. The train had wheels.
4. The wheels glinted in the sun.
5. The wheels squeaked.
6. The wheels strained.
7. The straining was under their load.

1. *The earth revolves around the sun.*
2. The revolution is every 365¼ days.
3. *The earth rotates on its axis.*
4. The rotation is every 24 hours.
5. The revolution gives us years.
6. The rotation gives us days.

1. *Pedestrians scramble across the street.*
2. Pedestrians stumble toward safety.
3. Safety is on the curb.
4. Their heads are bobbing.
5. Their faces are nervous.

1. The boy wore a jacket.
2. The jacket was faded.
3. The jacket was of denim.
4. The boy wore jeans.
5. The jeans were blue.
6. *The boy paused near the counter.*
7. The counter was for tickets.
8. The boy looked at the schedule.
9. The boy shifted his weight.
10. The shifting was from foot to foot.

1. *Nurses must study.*
2. The nurses are registered.
3. The studying is for at least two years.
4. Nurses take courses.
5. Nurses interne.
6. The interning is in hospitals.
7. *Nurses must pass an examination.*
8. The examination is state.
9. Nurses must demonstrate.
10. The demonstration is of their knowledge.
11. The demonstration is of their competence.

and

1. *A crankshaft converts combustion into torque.*
2. Torque is mechanical energy.
3. The energy is transferred to the axle.
4. The axle is in the rear.
5. The transfer makes the vehicle move.

1. The arena is grotesque. ·
2. The arena is monolithic.
3. The arena is for sports.
4. *The arena squats in the desert.*
5. The arena has walls.
6. The walls are concrete.
7. The walls lift out of the sand.
8. The walls are gray.
9. The walls are curved like a bowl.
10. The arena is a monument.
11. The monument is to the athletic department.

1. *Three girls were lying on the grass.*
2. The girls were suntanned.
3. The girls were eating sandwiches.
4. The girls were sipping milkshakes.
5. The milkshakes were chocolate.
6. The girls were watching the boys.
7. The boys swaggered down the walk.
8. The boys flexed their muscles.
9. The muscles were from playing football.

1. The students are anxious.
2. The anxiety is to record ideas.
3. The ideas are the teacher's.
4. *The students wait.*
5. Their pencils are poised.
6. The students are ready.
7. The readiness is to write down the words.

1. The captain is thick-shouldered.
2. The captain is built like a wedge.
3. He is captain of the team.
4. *The captain stands at the sidelines.*
5. The captain leans toward the microphone.
6. The captain grins.
7. The captain speaks words.
8. The words echo through the bleachers.

1 *Our minds are often transported.*
2. The transporting is by music.
3. Our minds are carried to a place.
4. The place is far from reality.
5. The place is a kind of sanctuary.
6. The sanctuary is where we can think.

1. *Tornadoes often occur.*
2. The occurrence is in Kansas.
3. Tornadoes demolish buildings.
4. Tornadoes destroy crops.
yet 5. Tornadoes injure people.
6. *The damage is far less.*
7. Tornadoes do damage.
8. Accidents do damage.
9. The accidents are from automobiles.
10. The damage is in a single weekend.
11. The accidents are on highways.
12. The highways are in Kansas.

Another Fable

1. Seagulls circle.
2. The circling is in the dawn.
3. The dawn is drizzling.
4. The dawn is gray.
5. *Seagulls lift.*
6. The seagulls are young.
7. *Seagulls soar.*
8. Seagulls extend their wings.
9. The extension is into the wind.
10. The wind is in the morning.

11. *They are just in time.*
12. The time is for flying school.
13. Flying school has a purpose.
14. The purpose is to teach them.
15. The teaching is about the boats.
16. The teaching is about the docks.

17. "Stay close!
18. "The closeness is to shore."
19. *A bird cries.*
20. The bird is old.
21. The bird dips a wing.
22. The wing is dirty.
23. "Food floats close in!"

24. "Don't dream!"
25. *The seagull says.*
26. The seagull is old.
27. "The dream would be to wheel.
28. "Wheeling would be free.
29. "Wheeling would be high.
30. "Wheeling would be above the sea.
31. "The sea is open.
32. "The sea is rolling."

33. "Gulls must live close in!
34. "The living is in flocks.
35. "The closeness is to docks.
36. "Docks are for fishing."

37. The class follows the teacher.
  ⌐38. *The class breaks up.*
  │ 39. The class swoops.
but 40. The swooping is toward the shore.
  └41. *One bird remains.*
42. The bird is white.
43. The bird remembers his dream.

Magic Words

1. *Words seem to have power.*
2. The power is magic.
3. The power controls behavior.
4. The behavior is ours.

5. Some words are vulgar.
6. Some words are profane.
7. *Some words cause blushes.*
8. Some words create situations.
9. The situations are embarrassing.
10. The situations are humorous.
11. The humor is occasional.

12. Some words are angry.
13. Some words are insulting.
14. *Some words result in conflicts.*
15. The conflicts are physical.
16. Some words generate tensions.
17. The generating is sometimes.
18. The tensions lead to wars.

19. Some words are religious.
20. *Some words bind people.*
21. The binding is solemn.
22. The binding is together.

whereas

23. The binding is in marriage.
24. Other words are legal.
25. *Other words separate people.*
26. The separation is through divorce.
27. Other words nullify vows.
28. The vows were for marriage.

29. Some words are abstract.
30. *Some words become causes.*
31. Men die for causes.

32. *Still other words are tender.*
33. *Still other words help people.*
34. The help is to overcome loneliness.
35. The help is to show love.

Final Exam

1. *She sat at her desk.*
2. She chewed her fingernails.
3. The chewing was nervous.
4. She stared at the exam.
5. The exam was a final.
6. The exam was in her course.
7. The course was sociology.

8. *The room seemed hot.*
9. The air was humid.
10. The air was stuffy.

11. She looked up.
12. *She saw her instructor.*
13. The instructor moved around his desk.
14. The instructor had a coat.
15. The coat was off.
16. The sleeves were rolled up.
17. A smile was on his face.
18. The smile was grim.

19. *A buzzer sounded.*
20. The buzzer was a warning.
21. The sound was down the hall.
22. *She felt her insides.*
23. Her insides trembled.
24. The trembling was from fear.

     25. *She swallowed the dryness.*
     26. The dryness was unnatural.

and 27. The dryness was in her mouth.
     28. *She glanced at the exam.*
     29. The words swam.
     30. The swimming was before her eyes.

31. *She had prepared for the exam.*
32. She had attended class.
33. She had taken notes.
34. She had done the assignments.
35. She had reviewed.
36. The review was careful.
37. The review was for the text.

38. *But his directions had caught her.*
39. The catching was by surprise:
40. "Write yourself a question.
41. "The question should be important.
42. "Answer the question."

Starting the Car

1. *Mac pressed the button.*
2. The button was chrome.
3. *Mac pulled at the handle.*
4. The handle was on the door.
5. The handle was a curve.
6. The curve was hot.
7. The heat was under his palm.

8. *The door swung open.*
9. The door squeaked on its hinge.
10. The hinge was worn.

11. Mac slid into the seat.
12. The seat was in front.
13. *Mac arched his back.*
14. The arching was away from the upholstery.
15. Mac rolled down the window in turns.
16. The turns were forward.
17. The turns were jerky.

18. *The glare made Mac frown.*
19. The glare was blinding.
20. The glare was of sunlight.

21. *Mac fumbled the key into the ignition.*
22. Mac pumped the gas pedal.
23. *Mac listened to the growl.*
24. The growl was of gears.
25. The gears were in the starter.
26. Mac listened to the suck.
27. The suck was of gas.
28. Mac listened to the strain.
29. The strain was of the engine.
30. The engine had parts.
31. The parts worked in harmony.
32. The harmony was mechanical.
33. The parts turned.
34. The parts stroked.
35. The parts lifted against the spark.
36. The spark was hesitant.

37. *The engine coughed once.*
38. The engine sputtered against its own turning.
39. The engine died.

40. *Mac felt sweat.*
41. The sweat dampened his armpits.

42. *The engine coughed again.*
43. *The engine died again.*

44. Mac had fingers.

┌ **45.** *The fingers twisted the key once more.*
and **46.** The fingers tightened with nervousness.
└ **47.** *This time the engine wheezed to life.*

48. The exhaust puffed out a cloud.

49. The cloud was smoke.

50. The smoke was blue.

51. The smoke soiled the air.

┌ **52.** *Mac pressed the pedal.*
and **53.** The pedal was for gas.
└ **54.** *The car swerved.*

55. *The tire was flat.*

56. The tire was in back.

57. *Mac spoke.*

58. "Damn."

Child of Technology

1. It stands in the lobby.

and ┌ **2.** *It hums.*
└ **3.** *It glows.*

4. It waits for food.

5. Food is in a form.

6. The form is coins.

7. It has a body.
8. *The body is lined.*
9. The lining is with buttons.
10. The body is metallic.
11. The body is brown.
12. It has a face.
13. The face is tattooed.
14. The tattooing is with ads.
15. The ads are for drinks.

16. It is like a sentry.
17. It is watchful.
18. It is waiting.
19. *It is ready to respond.*
20. The response is to a touch.
21. The touch belongs to the customer.
22. The response is for a price.

23. *It is the machine.*
24. The machine is for pop.
25. It is a child.
26. The child is of technology.

27. *This machine gobbles coins.*
28. The gobbling is eager.
29. The gobbling is to sustain itself.
30. The machine rarely spits the coins back.

31. *Often it has indigestion.*
32. The indigestion is mechanical.
33. It refuses to respond.
34. It refuses to serve drinks.
35. It remains indifferent.
36. The indifference is to threats.
37. The indifference is to curses.
38. The indifference is to kicks.
39. The kicks are violent.

40. *Technology may be good.*
41. The goodness is for indifference.
but 42. The indifference is mechanical.
43. *People are more fun.*
44. People make a difference.

Departure

1. *The apartment was quiet.*
2. Ticking punctuated the quiet.
3. The ticking was insistent.
4. The ticking was soft.
5. The ticking came from a clock.
6. The clock had a face.
7. The face was round.
8. The face was lonely.

9. *All the boxes were stacked.*
10. The stacking was neat.
11. The boxes were of cardboard.
12. The stacking was in the corner.
13. The corner was out of the way.

14. *Inside were books.*
15. *Inside were papers.*
16. The books represented hours.
17. The papers represented hours.
18. The hours were of study.

19. Sharon sipped a glass.
20. The glass held wine.
21. *Sharon padded across the room.*
22. The room was bare.
23. *Sharon sat down.*
24. Sharon leaned against the boxes.
25. Sharon's eyes were closed.
26. The closing shut off tears.

27. *An hour passed.*
28. The passing was punctuated.
29. The punctuation was by ticking.
30. The ticking was from the clock.

31. *Then she heard a honk.*
32. The honk was in the lot.
33. The lot was for parking.
34. The lot was below the window.
35. The sound was abrupt.
36. The sound was impatient.

37. *Sharon glanced out the window.*
38. Sharon waved to the cab driver.
39. *Sharon took one look.*
40. The look was the last.
41. The look was at the apartment.

42. *The years seemed distant.*
43. The years had been there.
44. The distance seemed hopeless.
45. *The years seemed well beyond the rim.*
46. The rim was of her glass.
47. The glass was for wine.

48. *It was time.*
49. The time was to go.
50. The going was into the unknown.

51. *Sharon grinned.*
52. *Sharon raised her glass.*
53. *Sharon spoke.*
54. "Here's to me!"

FOUR RIDDLES

1. *It moves along.*
2. It works its body.
3. The working is over obstacles.
4. The obstacles jut from the earth.
5. It flexes.
6. It draws itself.
7. The drawing is together.
8. Then it pushes.
9. The pushing is ahead.
10. The pushing is slow.

11. He glanced up.
12. *He saw it.*
13. It was falling.
14. It was bright.
15. It was heavy.
16. It was like a fruit.
17. The fruit was ripe.
18. The fruit was huge.
19. It tumbled.
20. The tumbling was end over end.

21. Its wings were tucked.
22. The tucking was against its body.
23. *It clung to the stem.*
24. It looked like a predator.
25. The predator was out of the past.
26. Its eyes were bulging.
27. Its head was enormous.
28. Its head was ugly.
29. Its head was motionless.
30. The lack of motion was strange.

31. It works slowly.
32. It works without noise.
33. *It begins to change the face.*
34. The change is from "no."
35. The change is to "yes."
and 36. It erases the tiredness.
37. It erases the wrinkles.
38. *It begins to change the soul.*
39. It dispels pessimism.
40. It makes the world cheerful.

Term Paper

1. *The writer pauses.*
2. The writer turns phrases.
3. The writer turns words.
4. The writer turns possibilities.
5. The possibilities are for organization.
6. The turning is in his mind.

7. *Things seem confused.*
8. Things seem muddled.
9 The muddling is hopeless.
10. Things seem without direction.

11. *Notes litter the table.*
12. The women average a salary.
13. The table is for work.
14. The notes wait to be assembled.
15. The assembly is into a structure.
16. The structure is well built.
17. The structure is logical.
18. The structure is worthwhile.

19. *The writer stares at the notes.*
20. The notes result from work.
21. The work was in the library.
22. The writer tries to imagine a design.
23. The design is coherent.
24. The design is a blueprint.
25. The blueprint is for writing.

26. Questions echo over and over.
27. *Questions reverberate in the writer's mind.*
28. The questions are familiar.
29. The questions press for a plan.
30. The plan is simple.
31. The plan is workable.

32. *And then something happens.*
33. The something is strange.

34. *The writer gets a glimmer.*
35. The glimmer is an idea.
36. The idea is for organization.

37. *The writer knows.*
38. The knowledge is of a birth.
39. The birth is about to happen.
40. The birth is of a term paper.

Red Power

1. *A feeling seems to be growing.*
2. The feeling is nationalism.
3. The nationalism is Indian.
4. The feeling is uniting tribes.
5. The tribes are diverse.

6. The movement has been promoted.
7. The promotion is done by Indians.
8. The Indians are young.
9. The Indians are well educated.
10. *The movement seeks ends.*
11. The ends are political.
12. The ends are social.
13. The ends include reforms.
14. The reforms would be in education.
15. The reforms would be in housing.
16. The reforms would be in health.
17. The reforms would be in development.
18. The development would be economic.
19. The development would be on the reservations.

20. The spirit bears similarities.
21. The similarities are to other movements.
22. The movements are of minorities.
23. *The spirit is militant.*
24. The militancy is firm.
25. The spirit is one of self-determination.
26. Self-determination would be for Indian affairs.

27. *The struggle is to assume some control.*
28. The Bureau of Indian Affairs would be controlled.
29. The BIA is an agency.
30. The agency is federal.
31. The goading is by anger.
32. The responsibility is for "paternalism."
33. Paternalism is an attitude.
34. The attitude is protective.
35. The attitude is authoritarian.
36. The attitude has been shown to Indians.

37. *Red power also struggles against time.*
38. It works to preserve traditions.
39. The traditions are cultural.
40. The traditions are tribal.

Women's liberation

1. Women's liberation is a movement.
2. The movement is political.
3. The movement is growing.
4. *Women's liberation seeks rights.*
5. The rights are equal.
6. The rights have been denied.
7. The denial has been throughout history.
8. The history is of the United States.
9. Men have denied the rights.

10. *Thirty million women work.*
11. The women are in the United States.
12. The women average a salary.
13. The salary is $4,000 a year.
14. The salary is half an average.
15. The average is of men's salaries.
16. The salary is for jobs.
17. The jobs are identical.
18. The identity is often.

19. *But men control employment.*
20. The control is usual.
21. Men force women to work.
22. The work is at tasks.
23. The tasks are menial.
24. Men reserve positions.
25. The positions are executive.
26. The positions wield power.
27. The reservation is for themselves.

28. *Education provides an example.*
29. The example is clear.
30. The example is of status.
31. The status is reduced.
32. The status belongs to women.

33. *Schools are administered by men.*
34. The schools are elementary.
and 35. The percentage is of schools.
36. The percentage is 80 percent.
37. *Schools are administered by men.*
38. The schools are secondary.
39. The percentage is of schools.
but 40. The percentage is 95 percent.
41. *The teachers are women.*
42. The percentage is of teachers.
43. The percentage is 90 percent.
44. The percentage is in elementary schools.
45. The percentage is 50 percent.
46. The percentage is in secondary schools.

Beginning a Review

1. *Invisible Man is a novel.*
2. Ralph Ellison wrote the novel.
3. The novel records a journey.
4. The journey is from innocence.
5. The journey is to experience.
6. The journey is from the south.
7. The journey is to the north.

8. *The hero becomes aware.*
9. The awareness is of his blackness.
10. The awareness is of his invisibility.
11. The invisibility is to whites.

12. The awareness occurs gradually.
13. *The awareness occurs through episodes.*
14. The episodes are seven.
15. The episodes are confrontations.
16. The confrontations are violent.

17. *The first is the "Battle Royal."*
18. The Battle Royal is a match.
19. The match is in boxing.
20. The match is staged.
21. The staging is for entertainment.
22. Whites are entertained.

23. The hero is blindfolded.
24. *The hero fights with other blacks.*
25. The blacks are his friends.
26. The friends have also been blindfolded.

27. The hero is goaded.
28. The goading is by fear.
29. The goading is by taunts.
30. The taunts are from the crowd.
31. The goading is by anger.
32. *The hero lashes out.*
33. The lashing is at his opponents.

34. His humanity is denied.
35. The denial is by whites.
36. The whites are sadistic.
37. *The hero becomes an animal.*
38. The animal is cornered.
39. The animal is fighting.
40. The fight is for its life.

41. *The hero is given a briefcase.*
42. The gift is after the match.
43. The gift is a symbol.
44. The gift symbolizes completion.
45. The completion is one part.
46. The part is of education.
47. The gift symbolizes a commencement.
48. The commencement is of self-awareness.

☞ NOTE: This review is incomplete. To finish it, the other six episodes would need to be discussed.

Quarterback

1. The quarterback crouched low.
2. The crouching was behind the center.
3. The quarterback glanced down the line.
4. The glancing was left and right.
5. *The quarterback barked his signals.*
and 6. The barking was sharp.
7. *The quarterback took the snap.*
8. The quarterback dropped straight back.
9. The ball was tucked.
10. The tucking was against his thigh.

11. *The quarterback wheeled.*
12. The quarterback dropped his shoulder.
13. The shoulder was his right.
14. The dropping was a feint.
15. The feint was to the halfback.
16. The halfback was slanting.
17. The slanting was off tackle.
18. *He pulled the ball up.*
19. His body rolled to the left.
20. He moved out of the pocket.
21. The pocket was blockers.

22. *His brain was alert.*
23. His brain was clicking.
24. His body was part of the flow.
25. The flow was beautiful.
26. The flow was action.

27. *He could see the halfback.*
28. The halfback crashed.
29. The crashing was into the line.
30. The halfback's helmet was low.
31. The halfback's body was crouched.
32. The halfback's knees were churning.
33. The halfback's knees were lifting.
34. The lifting was against the tacklers.

35. The quarterback glanced downfield.
36. *The quarterback felt his fingers.*
37. His fingers tightened.
38. The tightening was on the football.
39. His wrist began to flex.

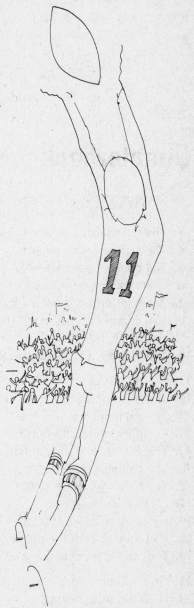

END

1. *The end was in the clear.*
2. The end was running.
3. The running was hard.
4. His legs were pumping.
5. The pumping was across the turf.
6. The turf was green.

7. *The image still lingered.*
8. The image was of his maneuver.
9. The lingering was in his mind.
10. The image gave him a feeling.
11. The feeling was of satisfaction.
12. The feeling was tense.

13. *The end had come across the line.*
14. The end had headed for the linebacker.
15. The heading was straight.
16. The linebacker was defensive.
17. The linebacker was burly.
18. The linebacker was dropping back.
19. The linebacker's hands were up.

20. The end had faked.
21. The fake was to the outside.
22. *The end had slowed down.*
23. The end had glanced back.
24. Then the end had spurted.
25. The·spurting was sudden.
26. The spurting was up the middle.
27. The spurting was toward the safety.
28. The end had left the defender behind.

29. *Now he was in the open.*
30. He angled across the field.
31. He watched the football.
32. The football lofted into the sky.
33. The lofting made a spiral.
34. The spiral was perfect.

35. His fingers were outstretched.
36. *The end strained toward the ball.*
37. *The end leaped.*
38. *The end gathered the ball in.*
39. The end heard the crowd.
40. *The end headed for victory.*